C0-ALA-881

Ski Cross-Country

SKI CROSS-COUNTRY

From touring to racing: an authoritative, up-to-date handbook

---

M. MICHAEL BRADY & LORNS O. SKJEMSTAD

THE DIAL PRESS • NEW YORK 1974

Photo and Illustration Credits: M.M. Brady: 2, 5, 6, 7, 78, 98, 153, 166, 204. NTB: 5, 218. Liv Skogen: 62. Jan Gunarsson: 80, 103. A-Foto: 106, 219. Spår-Kalle: 200. Studio 9: 208. J. Vaage: 212. Aamulehti of Tampere: 214, 216. Organizing Committee of the 1974 FIS World Nordic Ski Championships: 199. Otherwise all drawings by Eric Laukvik, and all photography by Frits Solvang.

Originally published in Norwegian under the title LANGRENNSBOKA FOR TURGÅERE OG KONKURRANSELØPERE by Grøndahl & Søns Forlag.
Manufactured in the United States of America
First printing, 1974

Library of Congress Cataloging in Publication Data

Skjemstad, Lorns O
Ski cross-country, from touring to racing.

Translation of Langrennsboka for turgåere og Konkurranseløpere. Authors' names in reverse order in Norwegian ed.
Bibliography: p.
1. Cross-country skiing. I. Brady. M. Michael, joint author. II. Title.
GV854.9.C7S5513 796.9'3
74–11138
ISBN 0–8037–6099–X
ISBN 0–8037–6079–5 (pbk.)

Contents

PREFACE

Until a few years ago, almost anything written on ski touring and cross-country ski racing in North America was prefaced with explanatory remarks. Fortunately this is no longer necessary, for American and Canadian skiers have become familiar with it, and ski areas are rapidly changing and expanding to encompass this traditional Nordic recreation and sport.

In many ways, ski touring and cross-country ski racing are unique among winter sports. They are relatively inexpensive compared to other winter sports. They can be done anywhere there is snow. They contribute more to overall physical fitness than almost any other games or sports, summer or winter. They cover an extremely broad range of human activity, from a Sunday picnic to an Olympic marathon. And, worldwide, they are by far the oldest and still most popular of winter sports.

Despite this widespread popularity, ski touring and cross-country ski racing have never been really well documented, even in Scandinavia where they are almost an indelible part of life. Coaches have been taught to coach cross-country ski racers, and ski instructors have been taught to instruct touring skiers, but little has been available to help racers or touring skiers themselves.

The original edition of this book, entitled *Langrennsboka,* was written to fill this void. It was published early in 1973 under the auspices of Foreningen til Ski-Idrettens Fremme, or "Skiforeningen" for short, Norway's major skier-service organization.

This English edition is a translated, revised, and amended version of *Langrennsboka.* The approach, scope, and content of the major parts of the book remain unchanged from the original, aside from a few facts, figures, and photos revised to incorporate or reflect developments of the 1973–74 season.

Some readers may find this book unconventional, for the approach and scope of parts of the material presented depart radically from most previous publications on the subject. This is not because the book is a collection of new and untried theories but rather because the material presented, although modern and recognized, has not been available before in print in English.

Technique as described here represents the greatest departure from that previously described in English-language publications. Specifically, it is modern Norwegian technique. It is an uncluttered, elegantly simple technique built around a set of basic principles used by both touring skiers and top cross-country racers.

This does not mean that touring skiers should ski like racers. It does mean that touring skiers can ski well by using the same basic techniques that racers use.

1. Modern physiology and kinesiology have shown that movements on skis are amazingly similar to movements on foot. Skiing *looks* quite different from walking, jogging, or running, which is why so many divergent theories and their resultant peculiar techniques have grown up in the past. But the basic rules of movement are the same. Thus the technique descriptions in this book concentrate on the similarities between skiing and natural on-foot movements.

2. Skiing is a dynamic activity; it involves movement. Thus each movement or stride is presented in this book as a dynamic whole built around a basic technique norm. This simply means that good technique, be it touring or racing, is *not* a number of static "correct" positions connected together, but rather a common basis for efficient movement that allows as much individual variation as desired. For this reason, there are no "positions" in this book, but rather discussions of movements—which is what ski touring and cross-country racing are all about.

Performing any physical activity well, or performing it at all, requires certain physical capabilities and condition, or fitness. The chapter on fitness and training in this book is aimed at touring skiers and cross-country ski racers. It contains basic exercise fundamentals and specific exercise programs for touring skiers and cross-country racers. These programs have been thoroughly tested; they are accepted by leading cross-country coaches and ski-touring instructors in Norway.

The chapters on waxing and equipment in this edition have been revised to present the range of products available in the United States as of the 1974–75 season. In addition, the reference sections on rules, race results, and literature have been updated, expanded, and revised for easy reference.

The authors wish to express their appreciation to photographer Frits Solvang for his understanding and continual helpfulness, and to artist Erik Laukvik for his illustrations, which were released through the courtesy of Gröndahl & Söns in Oslo. Specifically, they are indebted to the editors of Dial Press for the cooperative effort necessary for this English edition.

Oslo, April 1974

M. Michael Brady

Lorns O. Skjemstad

SKI CROSS-COUNTRY

1

Touring—The Universal Winter Sport

151
152

1

Touring—The Universal Winter Sport

One's complete awareness is absorbed by the skis and surrounding nature. It is something which develops not only the body but also the soul—and this sport is perhaps of far greater importance than is generally known.
Fridtjof Nansen, *The First Crossing of Greenland,* 1890

Beowulf is no stranger to students of Old Norse, who know that the Scandinavian Vikings and the Anglo-Saxons of the British Isles not only fought, but also met and talked. Many of the shorter words in modern English are Scandinavian in origin; "ski" is one of them. Modern Swedish and Norwegian each have from fifteen to twenty words merely to describe the skiability of snow—mostly for touring, the subject of this book.

Nobody knows exactly how skiing started. Snowshoelike footwear has been used in many parts of the world since prehistoric times. But skis, which differ from snowshoes in that they allow a glide on the flat and downhill, are uniquely Scandinavian in origin. The earliest known evidence of skiing is a forty-five-hundred-year-old rock carving of a man on skis on the island of Rödöy, off Norway's Arctic coast. Other archeological finds indicate that skiing spread from Norway to the rest of Scandinavia and the Northern Baltic some three thousand years ago.

Skis were originally simply for winter transportation, a method of getting around on top of the snow. At the time of the Crusades, Viking kings and peasants alike spent their winters on skis. While George Washington's troops were freezing in the winters of the American Revolution, Norwegian soldiers pitted company against company in open ski competitions.

These earlier skiers used simple equipment. Skis fitted loosely onto feet with simple toe straps as on beach sandals. Skiers had only one pole for pushing on the flat and uphill and for steering and braking on downhills.

Then, in the latter half of the nineteenth century, two things happened that changed skiing forever. First, Sondre Nordheim, a sharecropper's son from Norway's Telemark Province, invented bindings that allowed control of skis and skis with a side camber, or profile, that could be easily turned. Second, skiers started using two poles instead of one. "Modern" skiing was born.

After Nordheim's time, the use of skis as pure transportation diminished. Now only a few small groups such as the reindeer-herding nomadic Lapps of the northern Scandinavian peninsula ski in their daily work. The birth of "modern" skiing emphasized skiing for pleasure, recreation, exploration, and sport, which is skiing as we know it today.

Europeans and Americans learned skiing from Norwegian immigrants as recreation. They climbed snow-covered hills just to ski down again. Especially after the invention of ski tows and lifts in the early 1930s, this offshoot became very unidirectional: downhill only. It became known as Alpine skiing, to differentiate it from its Nordic parent.

Alpine and Nordic skiing are now quite different. Stiff, heavy boots fastened toe-and-heel to steel-edged fiberglass or metal skis are the Alpine skier's downhill locomotion; he must have a lift to go uphill. Light, flexible boots fastened only at their toes to light, laminated-wood or fiberglass skis are the Nordic skier's locomotion to go uphill, downhill, or on the flat.

This is ski touring, the all-ages, all-proficiencies, all-terrains form of skiing. It is easy to learn and enjoy, for it can be a stroll, a brisk walk, a hike, jogging, or running—as suits the individual skier. But it's more enjoyable with good technique, and with proper selection and care of equipment.

That's what this book is all about.

Racing—The Satisfying Challenge

Cross-country ski races are demanding and long. Some call it pain, others call it drudgery. Push yourself minute by minute, and keep it up maybe for hours. You sweat, you puff. You feel yourself "running out of gas."

Thomas Magnusson in the 1974 FIS 30-km race, which he won.

Touring is tops as recreation, even for those who otherwise could not enjoy skiing. Erling Stordahl, founder of the annual "Ridderrennet" race for the blind, races himself with a seeing-eye partner.

Is this healthy or enjoyable? Maybe not; for most it's better to stay at the recreational level.

But cross-country racing can't be judged as to whether or not it is "healthy" for everyone. For many it is definitely inadvisable. But for others it's a challenge to meet and overcome. There is something magnetic about the loneliness of the long-distance ski runner.

His may be an ordeal, but one that he returns to, even if only for the sheer satisfaction of having met a challenge—or of having finished a race only to shower and relax.

Preparation—physical training—for cross-country ski racing can be no easier than racing itself if it is to be at all successful. It must follow a regular schedule day in, day out—regardless of weather. It may not be everyone's idea of fun, nor should it be. But again the word is challenge and the benefit a feeling of somehow having realized a potential.

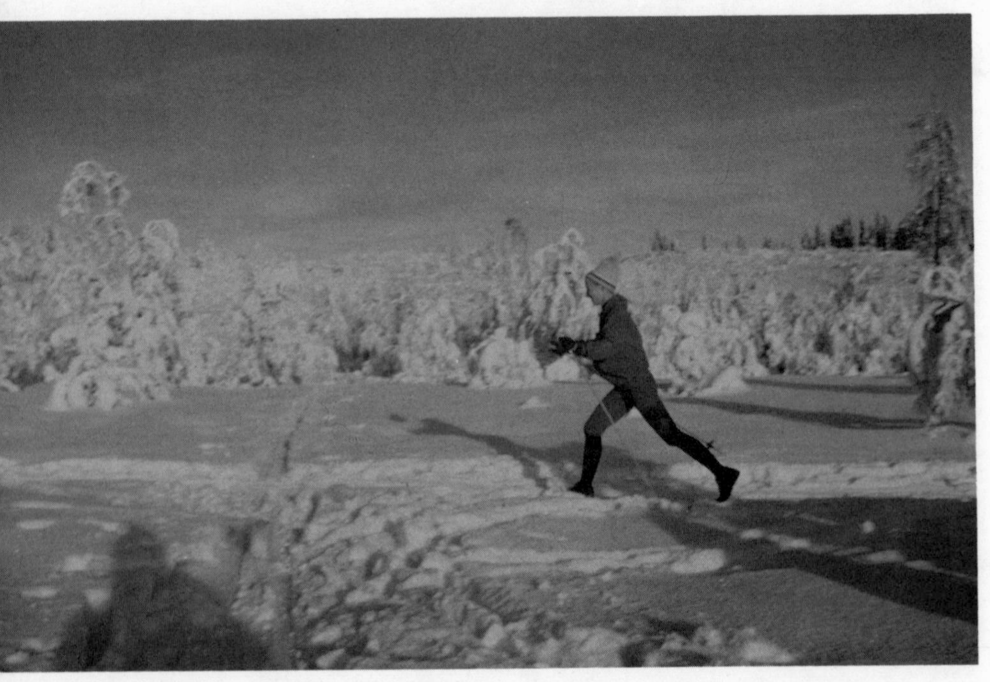

It's then that training becomes fun, even running in the rain and sleet of a cold autumn. All this simply because the reward is in sight—the rewarding feeling of capability and winter freedom following some wooded trail or crossing some plateau.

Skiing Physiology

Ski touring and cross-country ski racing use almost all the body's major muscle groups—arms, legs, back, abdomen, chest. Ski touring is, then, an all-around conditioner.

When major muscle groups are at work, the body's internal organs are also working at a corresponding rate. It can be strolling, jogging, or racing, or anything in between. But it's the activity that counts. No one activity can describe all forms of ski touring; each skier can seek his own level, his own fitness, his own thing in recreation or racing.

And Ecology

Some say concern with environment is merely a passing fad. But fad or not, there seems to be a very basic human need to escape civilization, industry, and the mechanization that man has created. The twentieth century may go down in history as the time when Western man realized that human success is not measurable only in asphalt, profits, or smokestacks.

On the other hand, there's no reason to return to the wild, to regress merely to suit hermits.

Ski touring has no parallel in winter outdoor activities. It can be done wherever there is snow. It's discovering a city park anew. It's skiing up a closed logging road. It's going directly to the next ski lodge. It's anything you want to make it. But most of all, it's the contact of man with his natural surroundings. Maybe that was Nansen's thought as he crossed Greenland on skis.

2
Technique

2
Technique

TOURING TERMS

Ski-touring technique has its own vocabulary of special terms, which will be explained as they occur in this chapter. But, for the sake of convenience, the most important ones to remember are:

DIAGONAL STRIDE Opposite arm and leg move together, as in normal walking on foot.

PASSGANG The lateral stride in which arm and leg on one side move in unison. Once popular when equipment was heavier, especially when skiers had only one pole. Modern lighter equipment and two-pole skiing have made passgang obsolete. Lateral movements are used only in the uphill tacking turn.

DOUBLE POLING Both arms and both poles move in unison.

KICK As in walking, a backward thrusting toe push-off and leg extension that propels the skier forward.

GLIDE The part of a ski-touring stride when one or both skis are gliding, partly or fully weighted.

GRIP Skis "bite" into snow giving foundation for the kick.

POLING Arm movements with poles that supply forward power. In touring strides, poling is divided into pulling and pushing movements.

WEIGHT TRANSFER Transfer of weight from one ski to the other. At a standstill, weight transfer involves only body weight. In motion, weight transfer also involves dynamic (due to motion) forces, much as those which allow a bicycle in motion to lean over in a turn without falling.

STRIDES AND MOVEMENTS

Ski touring has its own movements, each with a purpose. In this chapter each movement is described in terms of teach-yourself basics. Try each movement as you read, and then go out and try it on skis. Then go on to the next movement, repeating the process. Comparisons to advanced and racing technique are given for the advanced skier, who may wish to skip the basics.

If you can walk, jog, or run a distance, you can ski tour at the same pace over the same distance, whatever it may be. Ski touring in all its forms is similar to walking in all its forms. Your ability to ski well, be it a few yards or many miles, depends on your ability to cover the distance. Thus technique and endurance, or the ability to maintain technique over whatever period of time is involved, are related.

But to simplify things, technique will be explained by itself. Endurance can be whatever you now have, or it may be increased by physical training and exercise, the subject of Chapter 5.

Diagonal stride with poles is as natural as the poleless stride shown below. A good pack, as used on longer tours, allows completely free skiing movement.

Normal walking on foot

The basic ski stride is a normal walk.

Kicking a bit harder and leaning a bit more forward turn the normal walk into a good diagonal stride.

DIAGONAL STRIDE

Whenever you walk along a sidewalk, a trail or path, or even across your own living room or yard, you are using basic diagonal movements. Your opposite arm and leg move together in unison. The movements are automatic; you do them without thinking. This natural diagonal movement on foot is the basis of natural diagonal on skis and is why the diagonal stride is the most used in ski touring. It is used mostly on the flat and up gentle-to-modest hills.

The basic diagonal stride is easy to learn because it is *identical to your natural walk—nothing more, nothing less.* Any difficulty you have learning basic diagonal on skis will arise because you are unfamiliar with skis and do something that you don't do on foot.

Start practice on a flat snow surface. You should have a track, but if you don't, make one: Walk with your skis on, eighty or more yards in a straight line. Keep your feet about 5 to 6 inches apart as you would when walking on foot. Walk back and forth several times to pack down the snow into a solid track. Now you're ready to start.

Start simply by walking in the track without your poles. Walk just as you do on foot. Don't try to glide or go fast, just relax. The more you can forget that you have skis on your feet, the better. Relax your shoulders; let your arms swing forward and back.

When you are used to the basic walk, try to go a little faster. Speed up the same way you do on foot—by pushing off just a little harder and quicker with each step. The harder and quicker you push off, or "kick," the farther you'll get with each stride. You'll glide.

Take the first few steps slowly each time you start from an end of the track. Get into the rhythm; walk naturally. Then kick harder to get glide.

As you speeded up, you probably felt an urge to lean forward, just as you do naturally to go faster when walking or jogging. This forward lean is important, and it will help you even more when you start using poles.

Did your skis seem to swing up a bit in back as your kicking leg finished its stretch and the foot lifted off? Just like in walking

Firm but loose hand grip when arm is in front of body *Hand opens as arm passes body* *Fingers relaxed at finish of pole push*

where your leg swings up in back, it's a natural part of the diagonal stride. Don't try to make it happen; just let it come naturally, smoothly, and rhythmically.

Your movements should flow, as if you were walking to music. If you lose your diagonal rhythm, stop and return to one end of the track and start over again.

Thus far you've been skiing without poles to take complete advantage of your natural diagonal walking movements that you've been using since you stopped crawling and learned to walk as a baby. Most people need only 15 minutes of this poleless exercise; it's really that easy. Now take up your poles.

Start just as you did without poles. Walk slowly, swing your arms, hold the poles loose and don't bother with planting the poles' tips in the snow—just let the poles drag if it seems easier.

Now repeat what you did without poles; kick a bit stronger, lean a bit more forward, let your skis glide. Now use your poles—planting them in front of you, pulling down and backward until they pass your body, then pushing in back until wrist, elbow, shoulder, and pole are in one straight line. The movement should be almost the same as when you skied without poles; your arms should swing easily and naturally.

Uphill Diagonal

FROM FLAT TO SLIGHT UPHILL: Under ideal conditions, your first ski-practice track should be on a very slight uphill. This is because it's easier to ski diagonal up a slight grade than on the flat; the little extra resistance of the incline helps.

Diagonal stride up a slight hill

But you see and feel the difference in the *change* from the flat to the uphill. A rhythmic stride is easy to maintain on the flat or uphill, but a change in grade can be upsetting. Learning to ski these changes is an important key to mastering touring terrain.

Practice uphill diagonal on a track that starts on a flat and goes a few yards up a slight hill. Begin on the flat, at a comfortable pace, using the diagonal stride with poles and ski right up the hill. You'll find that your glide gets shorter and that you must kick a bit harder and push a bit harder on your poles to maintain speed on the hill. These reactions are natural and correct; you do much the same when walking up a similar incline on foot.

Try to suit your pace to the hill; get the feel of how rapidly and how strongly you have to kick to maintain rhythm. Otherwise don't change your flat technique. All movements are still straight forward and back, parallel to the track. Compare the uphill- and flat-diagonal-sequence photos above and on pages 12–13.

Refinements Skiing the diagonal stride on the flat and through a change from flat to uphill have allowed you to move on skis as you do on foot. Now for the few small differences that make the ski-touring diagonal stride quicker and easier than walking.

First, try finishing each kick with a decided straightening of hip, knee, ankle, and foot. This movement should be emphatic and quick. It gives you a little extra forward push, and it puts your weight in the right position to glide on the opposite ski.

If your skis slip backward when you try this full-extension kick, you are probably kicking only straight backward instead of partly downward as you do on foot. On skis, this pushing down is what makes the ski grip, giving you a foundation for your kick. Try again. The kick starts with a push down and finishes with a push down and back, just as on foot.

Slipping skis mean wasted energy, which tires. If your skis seem to slip more as you kick harder to speed up, try starting your kick a bit earlier when your kicking foot is still slightly ahead. The movement is very much like walking up a slippery hill on foot.

Do you move from side to side, do you waddle on skis? If so, you are probably kicking to the side, pushing yourself too far over the opposite ski. The stretching motion in your leg at the finish of a kick should *transfer your weight just over your gliding ski,* no more, no less.

Do your skis slap down in back, are you dragging your feet, are you shuffling? The shuffle on skis is just as incorrect as the

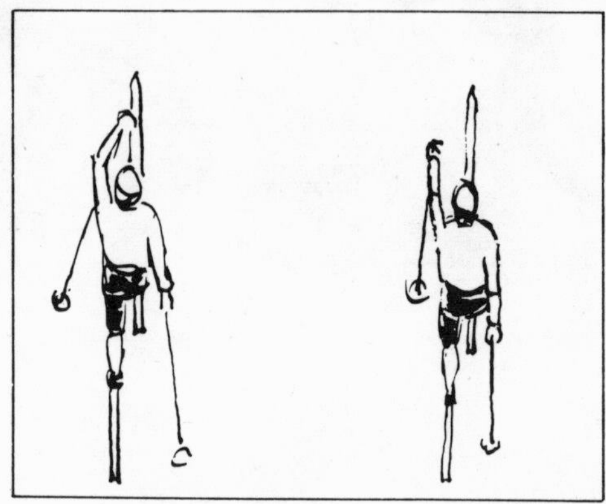

Individual variations but still good technique. Some skiers swing their arms slightly inward, while others swing their arms straight and parallel to the track.

shuffle on foot. If you shuffle on skis, you probably are not accustomed to the glide, which is the only phase of the ski-touring diagonal stride not found in walking. You should be able to glide balanced on one ski with neither pole touching the snow.

To cure the shuffle, concentrate on swinging your trailing leg forward with *no weight shift* until your feet are together. The leg that you have been gliding on kicks, and then weight is transferred to the leg that has just swung forward. Overemphasize no weight on the forward swinging leg if it helps. The rule for good diagonal stride kicking is: *weight on the kicking foot!*

Now try a few runs on your track going faster than the walking pace you've been using. Keep all movements parallel to the track —that's the direction you're going.

You'll probably notice that it's more comfortable to start poling with a slightly straighter arm as you go faster. This is natural. As your speed increases, each pole movement covers more distance on the snow and you need the slightly longer reach of a straighter arm.

But when you go uphill, your elbows bend more. This is because you move more slowly uphill and your pole movements cover correspondingly less distance on the snow.

Diagonal from Gentle to Steeper Uphill

Practice the same way as for diagonal from flat to gentle uphill. Your glide will shorten as the hill becomes steeper, and then it will disappear completely. But the kick and leg extension and the upper-body position are the same as for a gentle uphill.

The leg extension is essential to good uphill technique. Note that head, shoulders, hips, knee, and ankle are in a straight line as shown in the first, third, and sixth photos in the series on pages 20–21.

Wrong: Sitting position

Right

Go back and try the flat and gentle uphill again. Easier? More natural? It should be. You are simply learning to forget your skis. Don't worry about changing your stride to suit the steeper hill. If you are skiing well on the flat and up the gentle incline, then the stride changes needed to go up the steeper hill will happen automatically just as they would if you were walking up the same incline on foot. Each "step" will be shorter than on the flat and your pole movements will shorten—again, the same sort of change you would make were you walking up the same hill on foot, swinging your arms.

Your skis may slip backward. If they do, simply start your kick a bit earlier, pressing down on your kicking foot while it is still in front of your body. Avoid a crouch or a sitting position, which will only force you to bob up and down and waste effort. "Early" starts on your kicks plus more pronounced and stronger arm-poling movements will give your skis grip so you can ski straight uphill.

Herringbone

Your skis may have slipped backward when you reached the steeper uphill. It could be because your pole movements were not

Diagonal stride up a steeper hill. Rapid kicks are important. At the instant the kick is finished, ankle, knee, hip, upper body, and head should be in a straight line.

strong enough to make your skis grip well. Or you may have had too much weight on the last part of your kick and didn't transfer weight completely from one ski to the other. Or perhaps the hill was simply too steep to ski straight up. In any case, try the herringbone stride. It's not as fast as the ordinary diagonal, but it's far better than slipping backward downhill.

Try to ski the diagonal stride up a hill that gets steeper and steeper. Ski up until your skis start to slip backward. *Now* give your skis grip by spreading the ski tips apart, keeping the ski tails together so that your skis form a letter V. Roll your knees slightly inward to a knock-kneed position; this movement will roll your skis onto their inside edges, which helps them grip on the hill. Now simply continue your diagonal rhythm as before. The only difference is that you are now walking duck-footed uphill—much as you might do up the same hill on foot.

The steeper the hill, the more you must spread the ski tips, making a broader letter V to get grip. But as the V becomes broader, you may find that your skis seem to get in the way of your pole tips. Simply hold your arms a bit farther out from your body, and plant your poles in the snow with their shafts inclined backward so that the tips dig in level with or downhill from your boots.

Uphill herringbone, described on pages 20–21, is a diagonal movement.

Again, avoid a crouching or sitting position, which will make you bob up and down and waste effort.

DOUBLE POLING

Double poling means that both arms work in unison, swinging forward and back together. Double poling can be done with or without leg kicks or strides.

Strideless Double Poling Strideless, or "pure" double poling is used to pick up speed on the flat or on gradual downhills; cross-country racers often use it at the start and finish of a race. Their pole movements are rapid and strong; their double poling is the equivalent of sprinting on foot. But, like sprinting, this sort of double poling takes a lot of energy and cannot be maintained for very long, as can the diagonal stride. But just as you can jog without sprinting, you can double pole at almost any speed. The double-pole movement is almost always the same; it's just the tempo, or how rapid the movements are, that is different in touring from that in racing.

Practice double poling on a gradual downhill. If possible, both sides of the track should be well packed to give your poles a good bite.

The individual arm poling movements are very much like those of the diagonal stride, except that both arms work in unison. In addition, the upper body goes forward to throw weight onto the poles. This movement gives you a free push; your arms don't do all the work. Start double poling with a little speed, perhaps using some ordinary diagonal stride.

Start each double-pole arm movement by setting your poles in the snow vertically in front of you. Now let your body weight sink quickly over the poles by bending at the waist. At the same time, pull downward and backward on your poles. Feel that your body weight is always pushing on the poles. Your arms should then pass your body, and straighten to push on the poles. The pushing movement ends with shoulder, elbow, wrist, and poles in one straight line. If the movement is made quickly, you'll find it easy to finish each arm push with a little snap of the wrists, which

Double poling

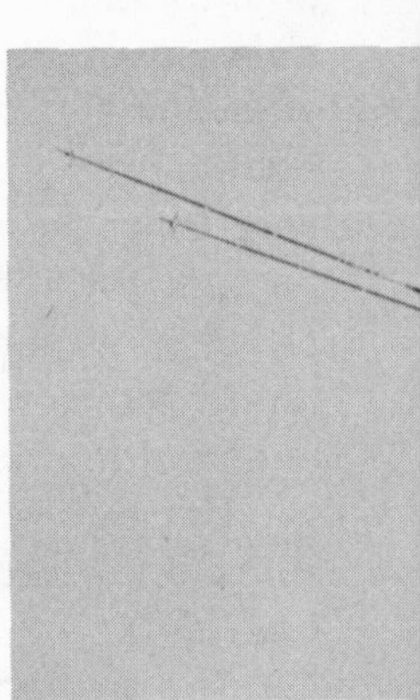

Double-pole stride with leg swing
Double-pole stride with kick

Pole *Glide*

Kick *Glide* *Pole* *Glide*

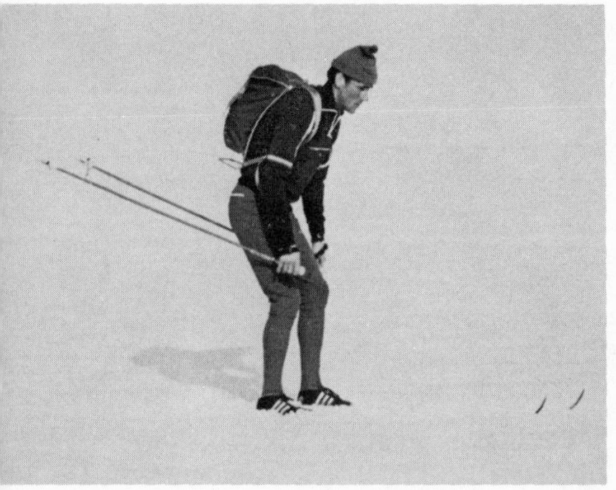

Touring skier double-pole striding

Racer double-pole striding

gives you just a little extra forward power.

Ankles and knees should bend during the double-poling movement, but you should not sit. Hold your poles with hands relaxed, and then loosen your grip slightly toward the end of the pole push.

Rise to a relaxed and erect stance after the pole push. Then glide with equal weight on both skis. Swing your arms forward with your hands open and relaxed. Some find this movement difficult; even top racers sometimes finish the pole push and swing their poles forward with the poles gripped slightly between thumb and forefinger.

Double-Pole Stride Perhaps you felt as if a little kick would help

when you were double poling. Don't resist the temptation; it's a natural movement. As the arms come forward, one leg goes back with no definite kick. The front of the body stretches fully before you bend over your poles. This double-pole stride is simply an ordinary double poling assisted by a leg swing.

The swinging leg can also kick to add forward power. Kick as the poles swing forward, as shown in the photo sequence. Change from kicking to kickless leg swings on alternate polings. This will give you a good double-pole stride rhythm.

The double-pole stride is the most individual touring stride; seldom do any two skiers do it exactly alike. But the basic poling and leg movements are common to all variations.

The poling is like ordinary double poling with no leg move-

More on Double Poling

(a & b) Skier gliding with skis equally weighted. Poles placed in snow vertically or inclined slightly forward. Arms extended forward.

(c) Pulling: Skier sinks over poles with a rapid bend at the hips while pulling downward and backward on the poles. Elbows are bent.

(d & e) Pushing: The skier follows through with arms extended in back. A slight wrist snap finishes the pushing movement. Double poling requires only a slight knee bend.

ment. Legs swing or kick once or sometimes twice between successive pole movements, moving as they do in diagonal striding. The kick starts with a slight sinking in the knee, is carried out with a weighted foot, and finishes with a straight leg. The straightening movement should be quick and complete.

After a bit of practice, concentrate on rapid and complete movements that push you forward—pole pulling and pushing and leg kicking—followed by relaxed forward swings. Both arms and legs swing up relaxed in back of your body after their forward driving movement is finished. Kicking should be as in the diagonal stride: in a direction to both drive you forward and place your weight over the opposite gliding ski. Between successive double polings, glide on both skis.

The similarity between the ski touring and the cross-country racing double-pole strides is shown in the photo sequences on pages 26–27. Both use minimum effort, but the racing version also aims at greatest speed.

STRIDE CHANGE AND STRIDE VARIATIONS

Stride change means changing from one stride to another, for instance, from diagonal to double-pole strides. *Stride variation* means individual style or alterations in a single stride, for instance, kicking once or twice between successive polings of the double-pole stride.

The skilled touring skier continually changes and varies strides to use terrain to his advantage, to break up longer periods of skiing with one stride, which can be tiring, and to best suit technique to speed.

The diagonal stride and double poling are the mainstays of touring technique. If you change between them and use different rhythms, you will gain a feel for the track or snow surface, much as you have a natural feel when walking.

(f, g, h, & i) Forward Arm Swing: The arms swing freely forward and upward after each push. Body rises to a more erect position, although at high racing speeds there isn't enough time to rise fully between successive double polings. Shoulders and arms should be relaxed.

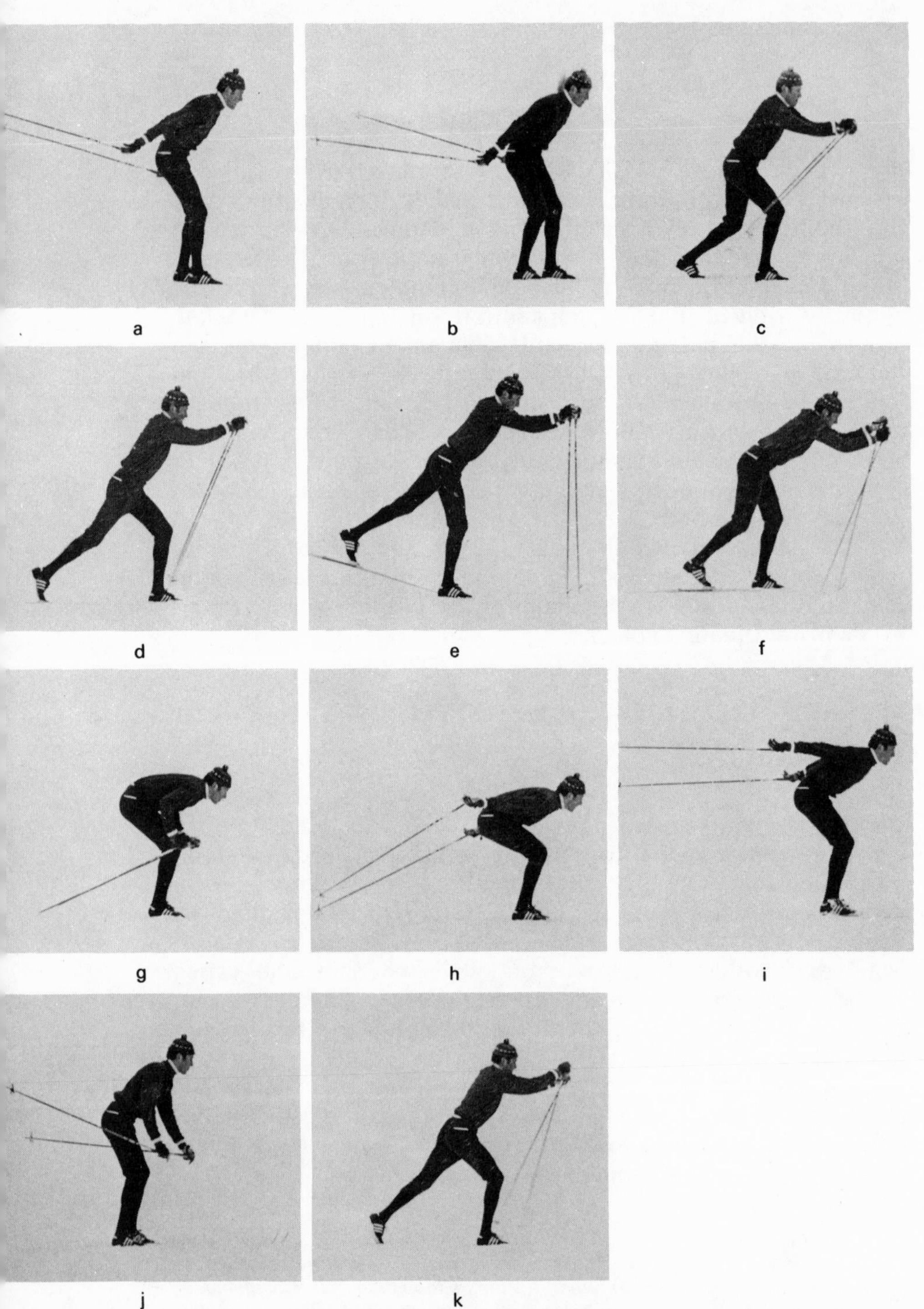

Double-Pole Stride
(a–d) Kick: The skier has been gliding on equally weighted skis before the kick starts. Some skiers start their kick from a more erect position while others are more bent over. But all have a rapid extension of the hips as the leg kicks and the arms swing forward, and the body rises to an almost fully erect position.

(e) Gliding on one ski: The skier glides on one ski with knee only slightly bent. Arms swing forward and up as preparation for the next double poling.

(f, g, h) Poling: The skier sinks over the poles. Note the body bend. The kicking leg now swings forward rapidly. Poling finishes with straight arms.

(i, j, k) Gliding on Both Skis: Arms swing up relaxed in back. The skier starts to rise to a more erect position, swinging arms forward, before the next kick.

Try changing from diagonal striding to double poling and back again. Start practicing this change by dropping a single pole movement every now and then in your normal diagonal stride. Once you've mastered dropping a single poling movement, then it's easy to follow by swinging both poles in unison, which puts you in the double-poling movement. On hills you can change from the uphill diagonal stride to the herringbone and back again as the hill steepness varies. On the flat or on slight downhills, you can change from double poling to double-poling striding with one, and then with two, kicks to each poling.

Each touring stride can be varied according to individual proficiency, height and weight, speed, and so on. The strides themselves can be varied, with diagonal-stride variations being the most common. Swedish racers have coined terms to define the different diagonal-stride variations. The variations are defined in terms of rhythmical "beats," or number of kicks executed for one complete set (one right, one left) of poling movements. Thus the ordinary diagonal stride is called the "two-beat diagonal."

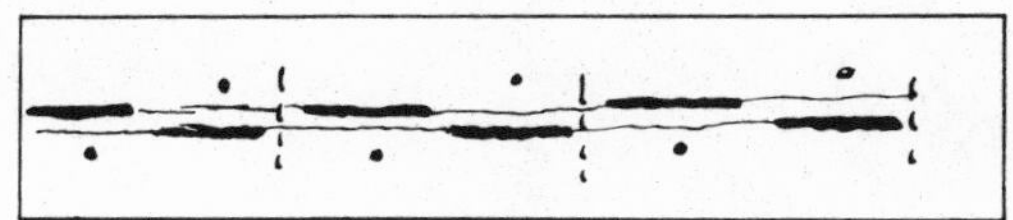

The variations are called "many-beat diagonal," with the two most common being the three-beat diagonal and the four-beat diagonal.

"Three-beat" diagonal stride

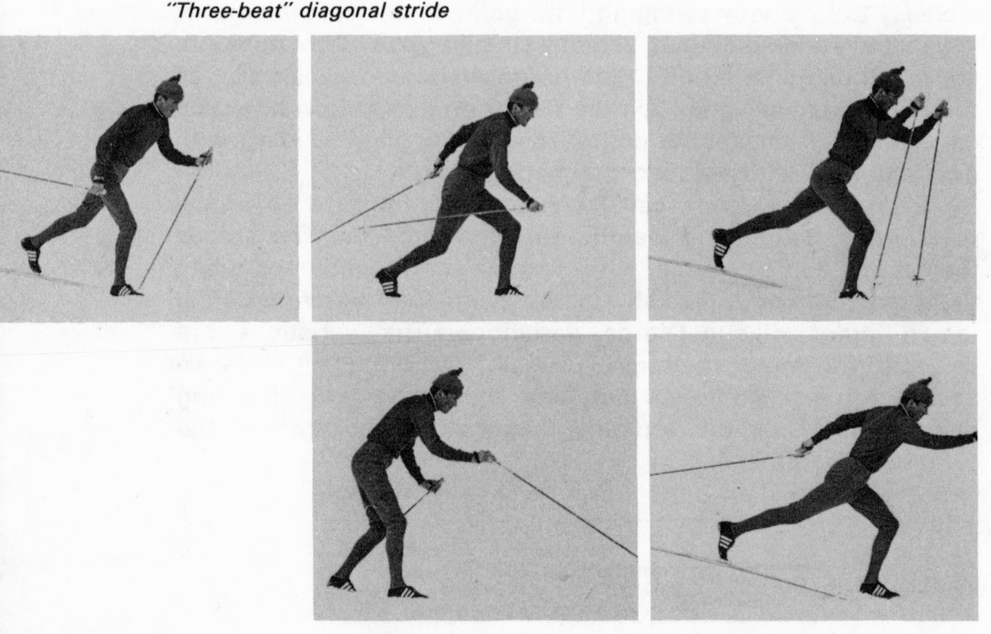

Expert touring skiers and racers use the three- and four-beat diagonal strides as variation from the normal diagonal strides. The technique of *not* planting a pole for these strides is to swing the arm forward and hold it there for the "missed" poling movement. The four-beat diagonal involves taking two extra steps—usually quite short—for every complete set of poling movements, and is most used on the flat in heavy snow or as a variation to relax arms when skiing uphill.

In German, the three-beat diagonal is called the "pendulum stride," which describes the pole movements involved.

FLAT-TERRAIN TURNS

There are many flat-terrain turns. The step turn and the skating turn are the two most easily worked into touring-stride rhythms.

Step Turn

The skis are stepped around to the new direction, one step for each double-poling arm movement. The steps are definite but have no kick. The step turn does not increase speed.

Skating Turn

The skating turn combines double poling with a skatelike kick, so it increases speed.

Gradual skating turns can be made without breaking the diagonal-stride rhythm; one "inside arm" pole movement is eliminated when the "outside leg" kicks into the turn.

Sharper turns can use several skating kicks before the arms double pole in the new direction. Long turns can have several skating kicks and double polings. Sometimes sharp turns are difficult in deep tracks. Then something between a step turn and a skating turn is best. The outside leg kicks, but not as much as in a pure skating turn.

1. The skier is gliding on equally weighted skis at the end of a double poling. The weight starts shifting to the outer ski.

2. The weight is now on the outer ski, the skier crouches for the skating kick, and the inner ski is pointed in the new direction.

3. The skating kick is finished, and the skier lands and glides on the inner ski in the new direction.

4. The outer ski is brought parallel to the inner ski, and skis are equally weighted before the next double poling.

SKIING BUMPS AND DIPS— "WASHBOARD"

Varying snow depths, wind, and skiers sometimes make bumps and dips or "washboard" out of snow surfaces just as cars often make washboard out of dirt roads. You can ski these irregularities without losing speed or stride rhythm.

Most bumps and dips and washboard are best skied using the diagonal stride or one of its variations. There are many ways to kick and plant poles, but there are no set motion patterns simply because there are no set types of bumps and dips. Following any set pattern only magnifies the roughness. A few rules should be observed, however.

Diagonal striding in irregularities is smoothest when the strongest kicks are made just after the middle of the kicking ski (just under the foot) has passed the top of a bump. This is when most of the ski is in contact with the snow and gives a good grip for kicking. Maintain your diagonal rhythm and kick naturally, with your other kicks—those not made just past the tops of bumps —being weaker. Pole to suit your diagonal rhythm. When double poling through dumps and dips, it's best to plant poles at the tops of bumps.

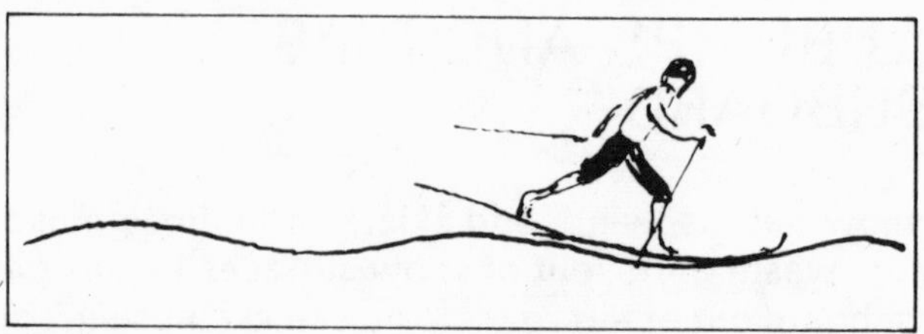

Don't kick hard in the bottom of a deep dip because the ski will not flatten out against the snow and grip, but will only slip backward. Worse, the ski may break.

But you can kick in the bottom of a dip if the dip is shallow, if the kick is necessary to maintain rhythm and speed, or *if your skis chatter because their wax is too thick.*

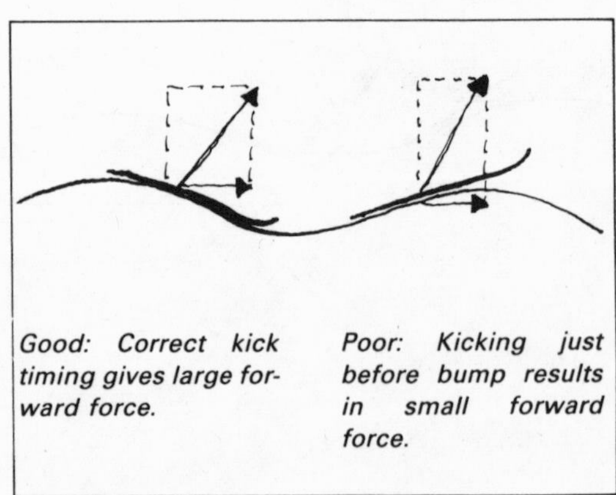

Good: Correct kick timing gives large forward force.

Poor: Kicking just before bump results in small forward force.

STEEP UPHILL

Traversing

Uphill traversing is simply an uphill diagonal stride at an angle to the fall line.* Edge your skis slightly into the hill by bending your knees slightly in the uphill direction. The uphill ski should point in the direction of motion, while the downhill ski should be more across the hill to give it a better grip. Kicks made on the downhill ski are stronger than those made on the uphill ski. Arms move as they do in the normal diagonal stride, except that it's sometimes easier to skip a few uphill arm polings or ski the three-beat diagonal.

Tacking

Skiing uphill on zigzag traverses requires a change of direction at the end of each traverse. The tacking turn, named for the zigzag course of a ship proceeding to windward, connects two traverses without a stop. The steeper the hill, the slower the tacking turn. It's always slower than the uphill diagonal on the traverse, but the main idea is to keep moving through the turn.

The first tacking turn shown is the conventional turn done in three movements in lateral stride (arm and leg on one side work together) with a shift from and then back into diagonal striding on the incoming and outgoing traverses.

Modern ski-touring and cross-country racing equipment is so light that many skiers prefer to skip many of the movements of the conventional tacking turn. In its simplest form, the tacking turn is merely a single skatelike step in the new direction, with no pole plants. If poles are used, the third pole movement of the turn usually comes parallel to the second in a double-pole-type movement as shown in the photo sequence.

A third tacking turn popular with racers is to ski the normal diagonal stride on the uphill traverse and shift to three-beat diagonal just when tacking. This amounts to skipping the inside pole movement in the turn.

---

*See glossary.

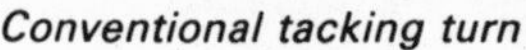

Conventional tacking turn

Racing tacking turn

Sidestep

Sidestep is, as the name implies, a sideways movement up the hill with the skis across the hill perpendicular to the fall line. The rhythm is: Upper pole and upper ski move sideways upward together, followed by the lower ski and then the lower pole. If your skis slip sideward downhill, edge them into the hill by pressing knees and hips inward. Compensate for this inward bend by leaning the upper body slightly downhill; the body then forms the "comma" position.

Poling rhythm can be varied according to hill steepness and snow conditions. The sidestep is almost never used in cross-country racing, but it is a reliable standby for steep hills and loose snow, as often encountered in mountain ski touring.

DOWNHILL

Touring skiers and cross-country racers use the same basic downhill skiing technique as do Alpine skiers. If you are already an Alpine skier, then your technique needs only slight modification to be useful on touring gear.

The basic rules for downhill on touring and cross-country equipment are: weight on the whole foot or even a little back on the heels, and "wide track" natural body position with the skis about two boot widths apart.

Downhill Running

The *natural stance* is the easiest and most erect body position for downhill running, but offers the most wind resistance. It's used mostly by beginners but also by expert skiers at greater speeds in uneven and twisting tracks.

Ski over bumps downhill by first rising to a more erect stance just before the bump, and bending your knees to "absorb" the bump as your skis pass over it. After the bump, rise to a more erect position again. Your head should follow a straight line parallel to the slope.

Sharp bumps and dips that throw you off balance can be skied using the Telemark position as used by ski jumpers. Advance one ski about a third of its length ahead of the other, bending the trailing leg so its heel lifts off the ski.

The *crouch* is the high-speed downhill position allowing the body to rest naturally in a position of readiness. It has only moderate wind resistance.

The *egg* is the position having the least wind resistance. It is a somewhat tense position of minimum readiness.

The main idea is to make the body streamlined. The head is down and the hips are up. However, because the egg is a tense position it is particularly unstable if you are tired.

A cross-country ski racer or a long-distance touring skier should rest as much as possible on downhills. But it's also a good idea to assume an aerodynamic position to minimize air resistance. The cross-country racing downhill position shown here lets the skier rest as much as possible while offering only moderate

Top left: The crouch allows the body some rest. Good readiness. Upper body as parallel to hill as possible. Good for downhill.

Bottom left: Skiing downhill over bumps. Head follows straight line.

Bottom right: Natural stance

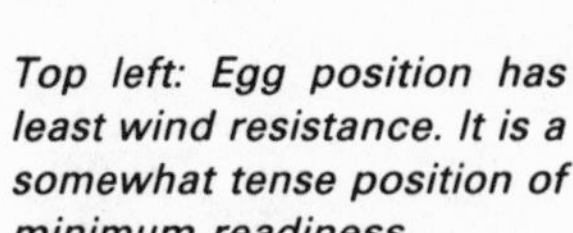

Top left: Egg position has least wind resistance. It is a somewhat tense position of minimum readiness.

Top right: Rest position is easiest and has only moderate wind resistance. Minimum readiness. Don't sit.

Bottom right: Snowplow position

wind resistance. It is not, however, a position of readiness, as the skier cannot absorb shocks from irregularities in the snow as well as he would if he were more erect. The position is assumed by leaning the elbows against the knees. Weight on each ski should be equal.

Stopping or Slowing Down

The *snowplow* is the easiest way to slow down or stop. With knees and ankles bent, press heels outward until the skis assume the plow position with tips close to one another and tails apart. Weight should be evenly distributed on both skis. Poles should be held with a loose grip and should point backward. The plow can be made more effective by spreading the ski tails farther apart or by bending the knees together, which will roll the skis more onto their inside edges. These two movements allow you to control the plow. Practice them first on a slight downhill, varying your plow and ski edging as you ski downhill.

Turns

Telemark Turn The Telemark, a steered turn common to older touring technique, has little, if any, place in modern touring. This is because modern skis are more easily turned than their predecessors and because the Telemark is basically unstable with today's shorter, thinner skis. Ski jumpers still rely on the Telemark *position* to absorb shock in landing. But touring skiers seldom use the turn and racers don't use it at all, except, perhaps, to show how it was done in grandfather's day. Experts can Telemark in deep snow.

Step Turn The downhill step turn as shown on the next page is similar to the step turn on the flat. It can be done with or without poling, according to your speed and the steepness of the hill. Poles really only aid balance while stepping. The body position is like that of the natural stance for downhill. The turn doesn't increase speed but rather slows you down a bit.

Skating Turn The downhill skating turn is similar to the skating turn on the flat. Poles can be used at low speed but are unnecessary at higher speeds. Start the poleless skating turn from the downhill rest position. Just before the turn, let your arms drop

Downhill step turn

back a little and transfer your weight to the outer ski. Then kick with the outer ski while pointing the inner ski in the new direction and swinging the arms forward. Assume the downhill rest position when in the new direction.

Plow Turn The plow turn is a braking turn most used for skiing slowly down a steep hill. The plow position is held throughout the turn. Weight on the right ski produces a left turn, and weight on the left ski produces a right turn. As in the straight plow, poles should point backward.

Downhill skating turn

Snowplow turn

Parallel Turns Parallel turns are downhill turns done with the skis parallel throughout the turn.

Wide-track turns are turns made with skis 4 to 15 inches apart. The wide-track position is the most natural biped position, so the wide-track turn is best for beginners and for experts skiing at high speed. The best place to practice is on a packed slope.

The turn is not difficult. Once mastered, it can be used instead of the snowplow turn. The wide-track turn brakes a bit, but it can be used for both sharp and long turns at any speed. When used with pole plants, wide-track turns can be done in a series of short turns. Long turns using the wide-track position allow the skier to maintain the best aerodynamic downhill position.

A long wide-track turn is the easiest. Simply transfer your weight to the outer ski and let your inner ski follow in the turn.

Short- and long-parallel turns on the same hill.

Lean your ankles and knees slightly into the hill toward the inside of the turn while leaning your upper body slightly outward toward the outside of the turn.

Sharper wide-track turns are most easily started simply by "pulling your feet up" as if you were on foot and about to jump straight upward. This movement is called unweighting and allows the skis to be swiveled to start the turn. Unweighting can be aided by a pole plant.

The inside pole of a turn—left pole for a left turn, right pole for a right turn—is set in the snow angled forward and slightly to the side. Plant the pole in the snow with a quick movement at the same time you hop slightly to unweight your skis. As the skis start to turn you withdraw your pole from the snow and weight your heels, pressing them toward the outside of the turn. This is called

Wide-track parallel turn is stable.

"turning power" but is really nothing more than a sideslipping of the skis through the turn. The upper body should maintain the same position throughout the whole turn—facing the direction of motion.

If you have cross-country or light-touring toe bindings, then you make wide-track turns with your weight slightly on your heels to keep them in contact with your skis. Heel plates on your skis, which keep your heels from sliding sideward when they are in contact with the skis, are a tremendous advantage for downhill turns.

As you become more confident in the wide-track turn, you can turn with your skis closer together. Skilled touring skiers vary the distance between their skis in wide-track turns to suit snow conditions, hill steepness, and their speed. The wider the track, the more stable and slower the turn.

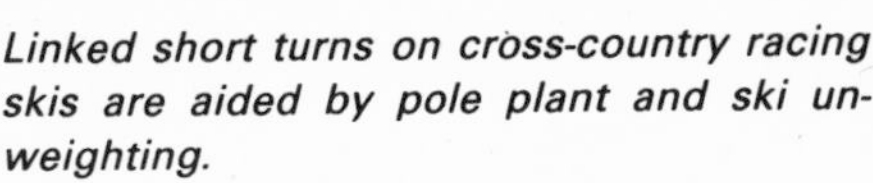

Linked short turns on cross-country racing skis are aided by pole plant and ski unweighting.

Linked Short Turns The literature of Alpine skiing is full of lengthy analyses of linked short turns, which won't be repeated here.

Basically, the skier faces downhill and turns in a zigzag pattern back and forth across the fall line. Each turn ends with a rapid edging of the skis, called "edge set." Just as edges are set, the inside pole for the next turn is set, the skis are "hopped" up to unweight, the heels are pressed toward the outer side of the new turn, which is what gives the turn its turning power.

Skating or Stepping at the Finish of a Parallel Turn A single skating movement at the end of a parallel turn can help regain speed lost in the turn or compensate for a turn that has been too long. But each skating step costs a bit of energy. For the racer, it's a decision of whether or not to trade energy for speed on a downhill.

There are many ways to step at the finish of a parallel turn. The most common step done by touring skiers and cross-country racers is an up-and-forward step at the end of the turn. Stepping is usually done to gain a better position for the next turn. Like skating, stepping costs energy, chiefly because it is directed uphill when the skier should be resting on the downhill.

Parallel Turns in Deep Snow Turns are best made on almost equally weighted skis. Let the inner ski initiate the turn and slightly weight the outer ski through the turn.

3
Equipment and Clothing

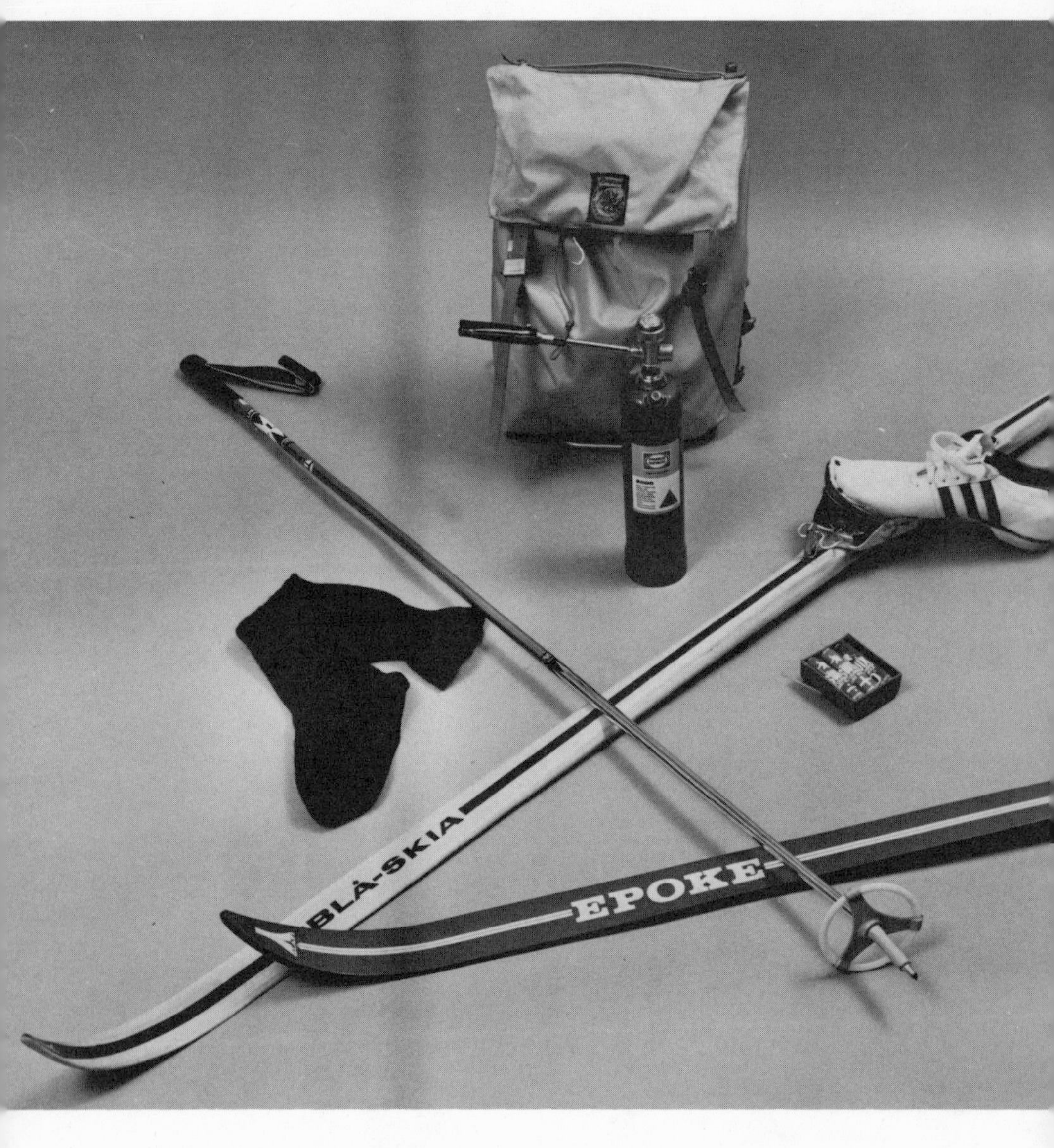
BLÅ-SKIA
EPOKE

3

Equipment and Clothing

There is no single "right" type of equipment or one "right" type of clothing for ski touring and cross-country ski racing. Equipment should be chosen according to skiing ability, the general type of terrain or tracks skied, and the usual length of tours. Clothing should be chosen to suit weather, length of tour, physical condition, age, and speed of skiing. In other words, equipment and clothing should fit individual needs, a ground rule for ski shops, instructors, and skiers alike.

At first glance, choosing the most suitable Nordic touring gear may seem a bewildering task, for the array of equipment is greater than that for any other winter sport. This chapter gives a few simple rules to make the selection job easier.

Ski touring and cross-country ski racing have virtually exploded in popularity in the last few years. From the equipment standpoint, one of the contributing reasons is that equipment is now stronger and lighter than ever before. But the strongest or the lightest equipment is not necessarily the best for all purposes. A long tour in mountainous terrain obviously requires quite different equipment than does a high-speed cross-country ski race over prepared tracks.

Prices may vary considerably within each category of equipment. Generally speaking, for similar items—laminated wooden skis, for instance—quality and price go hand in hand, because the market, especially the present growing U.S. touring ski market, is highly competitive. Nevertheless, high price does not always mean the best for a given purpose.

EQUIPMENT TYPES—EACH ITS OWN USE

"Touring," "competition," "mountain," "special," "racer," . . . and many foreign words—touring equipment seems to involve a host of terms and names.

In this book equipment is classified according to how closely it fits into any of three main categories: "cross-country," "light touring," and "general touring."* Cross-country equipment is the lightest, followed by light-touring equipment and then general-touring equipment.

The lightest cross-country racing equipment is intended for competition only. The lighter skis are marketed under names such as "racer," "special," "light," and so on. The sturdier of the cross-country ski types can also be used by light-touring skiers. But in general, cross-country skis should be used only on prepared tracks or on a firm, solid snow base.

Light-touring equipment resembles cross-country racing equipment but is sturdier and therefore slightly heavier. It is used by skilled touring skiers or skiers who ski only shorter day tours. Beginners can also use light-touring equipment on good tracks.

General-touring equipment covers a variety of ski-touring gear ranging from lighter equipment for all-around use to equipment resembling Alpine ski gear intended for extended high-mountain touring. The last category is often called "mountain" ski gear. General-touring equipment is well suited for beginners. But beginners need not be restricted to this type of touring equipment. A skilled beginner accustomed to recreational or athletic

---

*In general usage, as in the title of this book, "cross-country" covers both athletic and recreational activities. This complicates equipment definition: "light touring skis" become "cross-country light touring skis." The more traditional definitions are used here for simplicity.

activity can well begin on cross-country gear.

Jumping skis are also classified as Nordic skis as they are used for ski jumping, a Nordic competitive event.

Alpine skis developed from general-touring equipment. With the invention of the ski lift, it was no longer necessary to go uphill or on the flat, so heel freedom was sacrificed for better downhill ski control. As more and more lifts were built, Alpine equipment became more and more suited to its unidirectional use: downhill only.

In the days before lifts grew to huge gondolas reaching to mountain tops and before helicopters came to ski areas, many Alpine skiers climbed hills for the sake of longer downhill runs. They used special attachments to their bindings to allow heel freedom of a sort, and attached skins under their skis to climb uphill. As Alpine equipment became heavier and heavier and Alpine boots and bindings became stiffer and stiffer, this form of "touring" became more and more difficult, simply because a good deal of the skier's energy went into fighting his equipment on every uphill stretch. Although Alpine ski equipment is superior to Nordic ski-touring equipment for downhill-only use, touring on Alpine gear today seems illogical when good touring equipment is available.

SKIS

General-touring skis, light-touring skis, and cross-country racing skis are compared in the cross-sectional drawings on page 62. Most Nordic skis are still made of wood simply because the opposing demands of strength, light weight, and good skiing characteristics are difficult to meet with other materials. Fiberglass, for instance, is stronger than wood, but for its volume it is about five times heavier than most woods. Despite these difficulties, many good fiberglass and metal Nordic skis are available.

Until recently, laminated wooden cross-country skis were overwhelmingly dominant in racing, simply because they were lighter than fiberglass skis. However, in the 1974 FIS Nordic World Ski Championship races, over 60 percent of the racers, including eight of the fifteen medalists in the individual events,

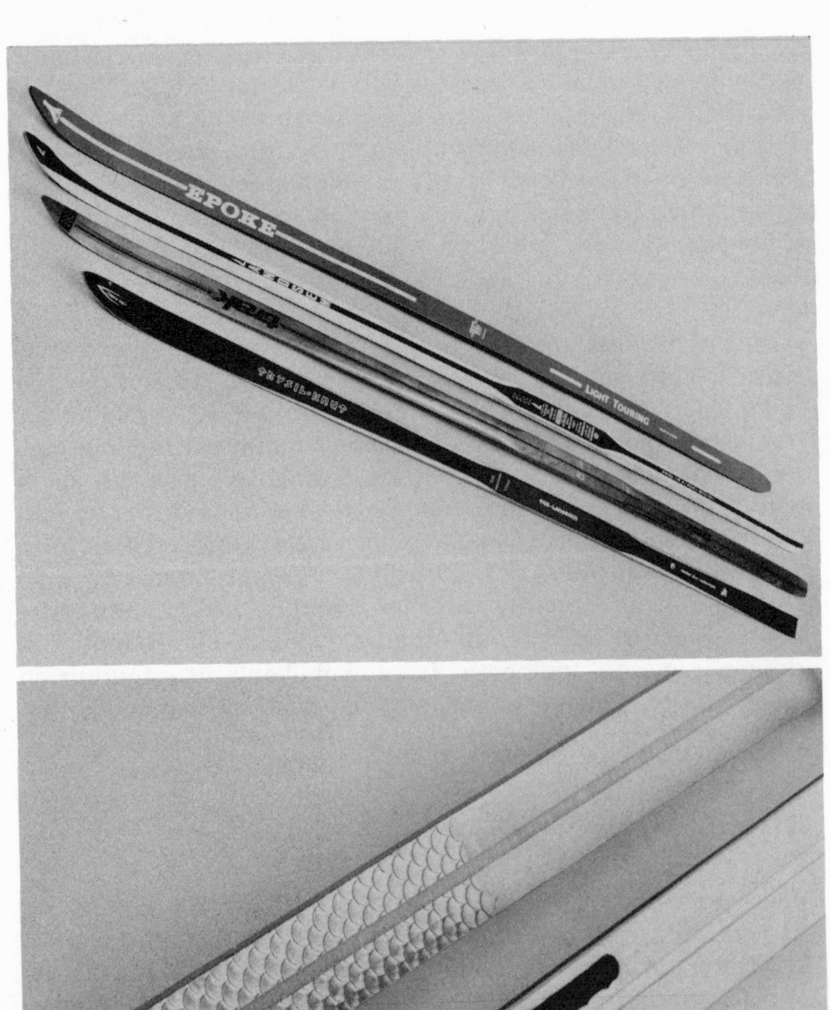
EPOKE
LIGHT TOURING

were on fiberglass skis. These skis were specially developed, high performance racing models. And like high-performance racing cars, these skis had disadvantages in general use. In particular, they did not hold wax as well as wooden skis for all temperatures, although they held wax better for restricted temperature ranges and snow conditions. Thus, unlike in Alpine skiing, where technical improvements are made first for racers and then for the recreational skiing public, fiberglass touring skis, available in recreational models for ten years, have now made it in racing. This success dictates increased popularity which means that their high price, a present disadvantage compared to wood skis, can be expected to come down with quantity production.

The general-touring ski is the strongest of the ski types shown in the cross-sectional drawings because it is broader and thicker and uses more laminations of stronger woods than do the other skis. General-touring ski bases are stronger and more durable than those of the other ski types and can thus tolerate more punishment. General-touring skis can be used in unbroken snow because their greater width lets them ride higher on the snow. However, greater strength and broader width mean that the general touring ski is the heaviest of the types.

Characteristics

LENGTH can be measured in two ways. Some manufacturers state length as measured along the sole of the ski from tip to tail, while others state length as a straight line from tip to tail. Thus a 210-cm ski from a manufacturer using the straight-line method will be about 3 cm (1¼ inches) longer than a 210-cm ski from a manufacturer using the along-the-sole measurement.

WIDTH can also be measured in two ways. Some manufacturers state width as measured at the ski's narrowest point approximately at its middle where the binding mounts, while others state the maximum width at the shovel back of the ski tip. The minimum-width measurement is the most prevalent and is used in this book.

Top: The spectrum of Nordic skis ranges from the stronger, broader general touring skis through the lighter cross-country racing skis.

Bottom: "Waxless" ski soles use either serrations or inlaid strips.

Correct ski and pole length depend on skier's height and general body proportions.

WEIGHT is stated as pair weight without bindings. As of 1974, a pair of 210-cm cross-country racing skis weighed about 2 pounds 10 ounces while a pair of heavier 210-cm general touring skis might weigh as much as 6 pounds 10 ounces.

STIFFNESS OR SOFTNESS in tip, mid, and tail of a ski indicate how much these parts give or rebound when the ski is flexed. A good ski springs quickly back to its original shape when flexed then released. The better the ski, the more it will seem to "flow" over bumps, the more it will "answer" a kick with a forward push. This is what skiers call a "lively" ski. Good Nordic skis have soft tips, are gradually stiffer toward the middle, and then slightly softer again toward the tail, with tails being stiffer than tips.

CAMBER is the arching of the middle of a ski up above its tip and tail. This arch is what distributes the skier's weight over the whole ski, although good touring-ski design places a bit more weight in the center of the ski than at the tip and tail. Camber is defined in two ways. Usually it means the distance between the two skis of a pair when they are placed together, bottom to bottom. Sometimes it means the force required to flatten the skis against one another. Thus, terms such as camber, stiffness, softness are related to one another.

It is important that each ski of a pair have the same camber. The best way to check for equal camber is to place a pair together, bottom to bottom, and squeeze the skis together to flatten the camber out. Sight along the skis from tip to tail and from tail to tip on both sides. The skis should come together in a straight line. When you squeeze a good pair of skis together, the last half inch of camber should be much more difficult to flatten out—you have to use more force. This is an important characteristic as it aids gripping and gliding in the diagonal stride.

Uneven camber, excessive camber, or inadequate camber all mean poor glide. The best camber is that which gives the best glide for the skier involved. A good check when skiing is to see

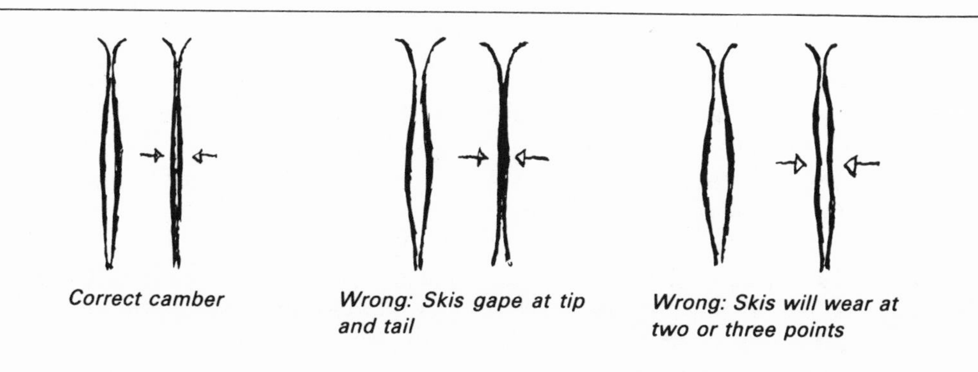

Correct camber

Wrong: Skis gape at tip and tail

Wrong: Skis will wear at two or three points

how wax wears. If the camber is right, wax will wear evenly over the whole ski. Excessive camber will wear wax at tip and tail but not in the middle of a ski. Inadequate camber will wear wax in the middle but not at the tip and tail of a ski.

As a general rule, select camber so that you can squeeze a pair of skis almost together with one hand and then flatten them together, squeezing out the last half inch or so of camber with both hands.

SIDE CAMBER is measured as the difference in width between the middle of a ski and its tip and tail. Side camber helps skis run straight when flattened against the snow and gives them control when they are edged. General touring skis have tips about ¼ to ⅜ inch wider, and tails about 5/32 to ¼ inch wider, than their mid-widths. The corresponding width differences for a cross-country racing ski are 5/32 to ¼ inch and 3/32 to 5/32 inch respectively.

STRENGTH usually means breaking strength and is generally stated for the different parts of a ski and not for the ski as a whole. Ski tips should be strong enough to tolerate running into bumps and resilient enough so that they can be stepped on a bit without breaking. The middle of a ski should be strong enough to tolerate being weighted in a dip without breaking. These different strengths are obviously less for a cross-country racing ski than for a stronger general touring ski. Fiberglass and metal skis are stronger than laminated-wood skis.

DURABILITY generally refers to the ability of the ski's sole and edges to withstand wear. Assuming that a ski is not broken, the most common reason for replacing skis is that their soles or edges are worn out. Hickory and birch are the most common woods used in soles. Hickory is stronger but heavier than birch, while birch holds wax better than hickory. Thus most general touring skis have hickory bases while the majority of cross-country racing skis have birch or plastic on birch bases. Edges are generally made of a material harder than the base itself. Birch-sole skis usually have hickory edges, while hickory-sole skis have "lignostone" (from the Latin *lignum* meaning wood) edges. Lignostone is beech wood compressed to half its original volume in an oil-impregnating process. Plastic edges are also available on some skis. Recently, some models of light-touring and general-touring skis have been made with composition-wood or treated-wood soles. Some skis are available with plastic or plastic-laminate bottoms. These synthetics are all more durable than pure wood.

Construction and Materials

Most Nordic skis are made of laminated woods, a technique originally developed fifty years ago to prevent ski warp. The laminating process is fairly expensive as woodworking goes. Only one-quarter to one-third of the wood used by a ski factory goes into the finished skis; the rest is chips or sawdust.

Laminated skis are composed of several horizontal layers, each of which has several laminations. There are thirty or more laminations in a high-quality ski. The horizontal layers are made first in production, and are then bonded together in a press that gives the ski its shape and camber. The top and bottom layers use the more resilient woods to make the ski strong, while the center laminations need not be as strong because they function as fillers and are not so decisive in determining ski strength. The more laminations, the stronger the ski and the greater its resistance to warp. Therefore the top and bottom horizontal layers generally have more laminations than the middle layers.

Some cross-country skis have air channels or balsa or plastic foam laminations in their middle layers to further reduce weight. These "lighter" laminations are generally used over only about half the length of the ski, centered at its middle; the tip and tail sections are the same as for heavier cross-country skis. Thus the only loss of strength is in the middle of the ski, not at the tip which is the most common break in cross-country skis.

The most common synthetic Nordic skis use fiberglass around a wood or expanded plastic core. There are two general types of fiberglass ski: the "sandwich" ski in which fiberglass sheets form the top and bottom layers of a wood-core or plastic-core ski, and the "wet-wrap" construction in which epoxy-fiberglass mats are wrapped around a core. A few metal Nordic skis are available. The most common metal construction comprises thin aluminum sheets sandwiched on an expanded metal or air-channel core. The bases of these skis are thermoplastic or epoxy.

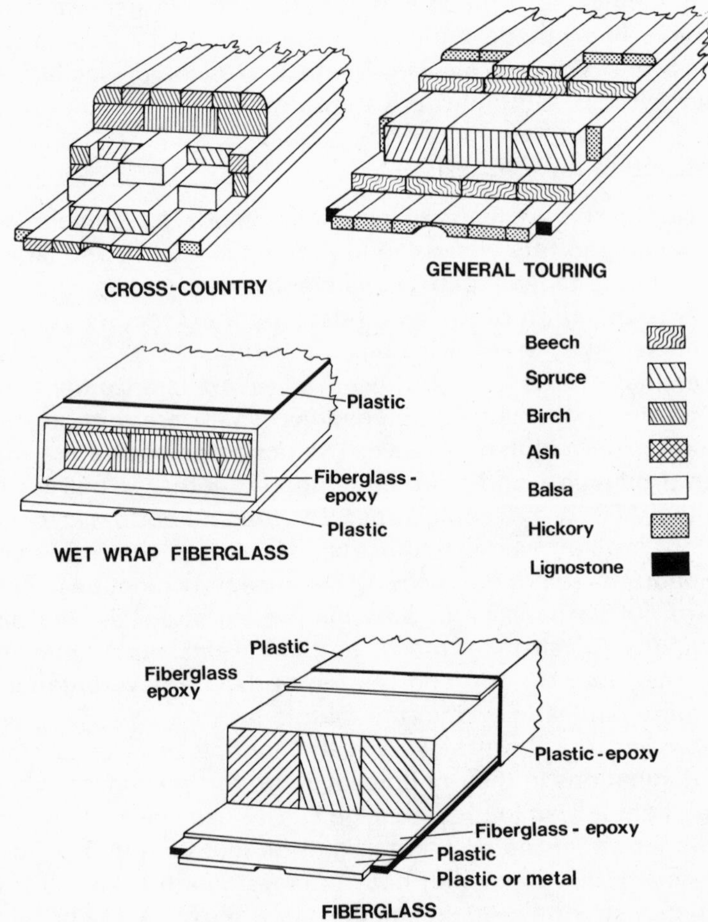

Cross sections of skis showing different constructions

Waxless Skis

Recently, touring-ski bases needing no waxing have been developed for recreational skiing. These waxless bottoms achieve their action either by serrations in a plastic base or synthetic hair strips inlaid into a plastic base. Generally the serrations run half the length of the base while the inlaid hair strips run less than one-third the length of a ski in its middle.

Waxless skis are still so new that, at this writing, it's difficult to predict how their future improvement will affect their use by touring skiers and cross-country racers. Thus far, no waxless skis have been used in racing, chiefly because for any given snow condition, their performance isn't equal to that of a well-waxed ski.

Width and Weight Differences Among Ski Types

Cross-country racing skis have midpoint widths up to $1\frac{31}{32}$ inches. They are the lightest and most supple type of ski. Their tips are extremely flexible such that they can move easily over all roughness in a track.

Light-touring skis have midpoint widths from $1\frac{31}{32}$ inches to $2\frac{5}{64}$ inches. The top and bottom lamination layers are usually thicker than those of a cross-country racing ski. Thus a pair of 210-cm light-touring skis is about 11 ounces heavier than a pair of 210-cm cross-country skis. Light-touring skis are strong enough for tours in mountainous terrain, and are now the largest selling type in Scandinavia.

General-touring skis have midpoint widths from $2\frac{3}{64}$ inches to about $2\frac{9}{16}$ inches. Their basic construction is the same as that of light-touring and cross-country skis. The combination of a softer tip and stiffer tail is retained, but because the skis are broader and thicker and use stronger woods, they are heavier and less lively. General-touring skis are light enough for most touring, yet strong enough to use for breaking trail. Their side camber is greater than that of a cross-country or light touring ski and almost equals that of a slalom Alpine ski. This large side camber makes them both steady on downhill runs and easy to turn. The broadest general-touring skis are sometimes called mountain skis. Mountain skis are ideal for extended tours in steep mountain terrain.

BINDINGS

There are two general types of Nordic touring bindings: toe bindings and toepiece-and-backstrap bindings, which provide greater stability for downhill running and turns.

Toe bindings attach the boot to the ski by clamping the front part of the boot welt to the binding. Most toe bindings have a toepiece. They differ from one another only in the way the boot is held in the toepiece. There are three general attachment methods: a bail which presses the boot down against pegs projecting upward from the toepiece, spikes that go through the boot and mate to holes in the toepiece, and "step-in" bindings in which spring-loaded clamps snap into metal pieces mounted on the boot toe. The Rottefella is the oldest of the peg types. Kloa and Bergans are examples of the spike type, while the Eie binding is a step-in type.

Toe bindings are now made in four standard widths,* all with the same toepiece side angles, and mount with three screws. Boots are made to suit these standard widths.

Toe bindings usually are mounted along with heel plates which dig into a weighted boot heel to keep it from slipping sideways off the ski. Some makes of heel tie-downs are available to provide extra heel control on downhills. With heels fixed to skis, however, the natural safety feature of the flexible toe binding is lost. In a fall, the foot can twist considerably around a toe binding with little danger of leg damage. With heels tied to skis, the entire foot is twisted if the ski twists in a fall, which can cause sprains or fractures.

---

*The 1973 Nordic Norm standard stipulates the four standard widths as 7.1 cm (2.79 inches), 7.5 cm (2.95 inches), 7.9 cm (3.1 inches), and 8.3 cm (3.26 inches) measured on a "transverse line" (through the rear two pegs of a peg-type toe binding). Older toe bindings sometimes were adjustable in width to fit the non-standard boots, and mounted with five screws.

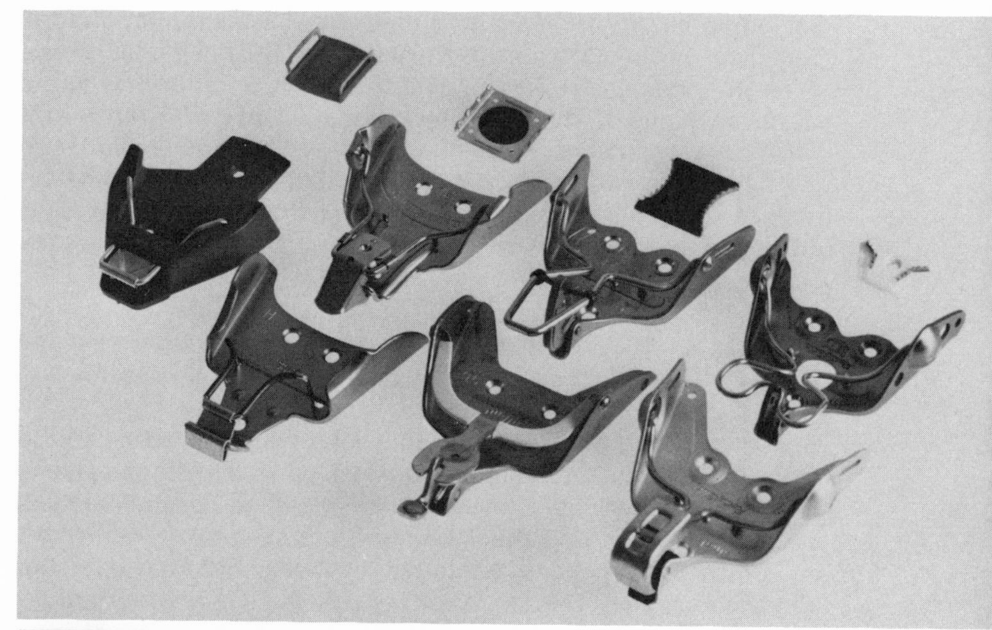

Top: Various models of toe bindings

Bottom: Toe bindings allow full foot freedom.

Backstrap bindings consist of a toepiece and a strap around the boot heel to hold the toe in the binding. The toepieces of the different bindings are similar, and the bindings differ only in the strap mechanism. There are two general types of strap mechanism: the heel cable with a front spring to provide tension, and the heel strap with a ratchet-loaded clamp to provide tension, both of which are adjustable. Some backstrap-binding toepieces are adjustable while others are available in fixed widths as are toe bindings.

BOOTS

Good ski-touring boots have flexible soles which allow the foot to "roll" over the ball of the foot in the kick while allowing full ankle freedom. However, soles should resist sideways movement which might allow the boot heel to twist off the ski.

Cross-country racing boots are the lowest cut and lightest of all ski boots. They are cut below the ankle like most men's dress shoes to give maximum foot freedom.

Light-touring boots are cut slightly higher than racing boots and usually have a groove milled in the heel for straps or cables for backstrap bindings.

General-touring boots are cut above the ankle and resemble hiking boots. They have a groove milled into the heel for use with backstrap-type bindings. They usually are made of thicker materials, which makes them both warmer than light-touring or cross-country boots and more stable on general-touring skis, especially for downhill runs.

Most ski-touring boots are made of leather because they must both flex and breathe. The softest leathers are used in the boot uppers so that the boot will conform to the foot and not chafe or cause blisters. The lightest cross-country racing boots usually have thin hide uppers.

Top: Backstrap bindings for touring

Bottom, from left to right: Boots for touring, light touring, and cross-country racing

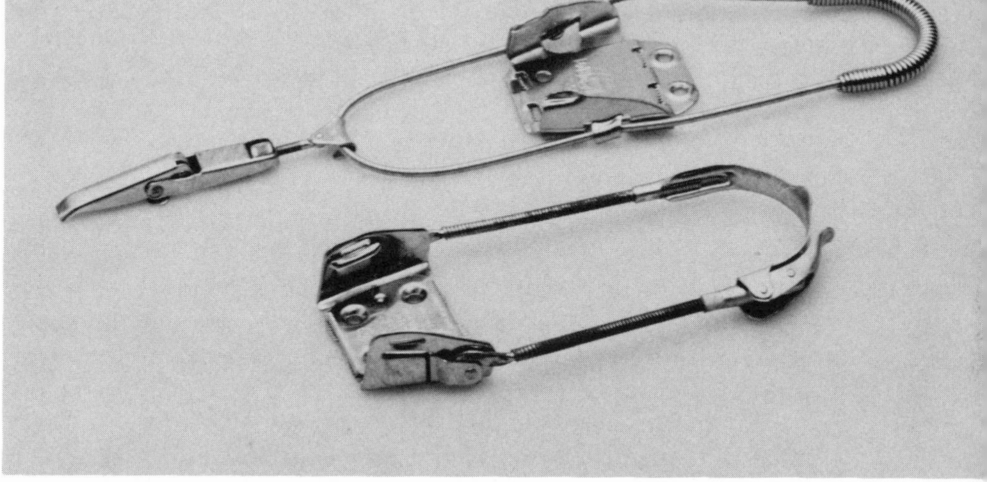

Many ski-touring boots have laminated leather-rubber, laminated leather-plastic, or injection-molded polyurethane soles, all designed to seal out moisture.

Some light-touring boots of rubber lined with synthetic fleece are available. These boots are ideal for spring slush skiing, and many of them are warm in cold weather.

Both leather and rubber boots are warmer if they are lined with wool.

Pullover Socks

The light leathers used in cross-country and light-touring boots are not good insulators, so keeping feet warm and dry in extreme cold weather may be a problem. Some skiers prefer to wear several pairs of socks, but this has the disadvantage that the socks may bind and rub or blister your feet. Pullover socks are an excellent solution to the problem.

Several models of pullover socks are available. Most are made of rubber, rubberized nylon, or nylon-terrycloth with rubberized toe and heel. These socks, which go on over your boots, should be thin enough to allow your boots to fit into toe bindings. Some skiers prefer the additional warmth of wool and simply make their own pullover socks from a pair of old ankle-high wool socks.

POLES

A good Nordic pole should be light, flexible, and strong. The flexibility should be just enough to let the pole bend slightly when planted in the snow and weighted; the pole should spring or "whip" back into a straight line when unweighted. Thus heavier or stronger skiers should have slighly stiffer poles than lighter skiers. The strength should be such that the pole can be bent well out of line without breaking and should spring back straight when the load is removed. A good pole is "lively."

Nordic pole shafts should be light, strong, and resilient. The shafts meeting these requirements are treated bamboo, or tonkin,

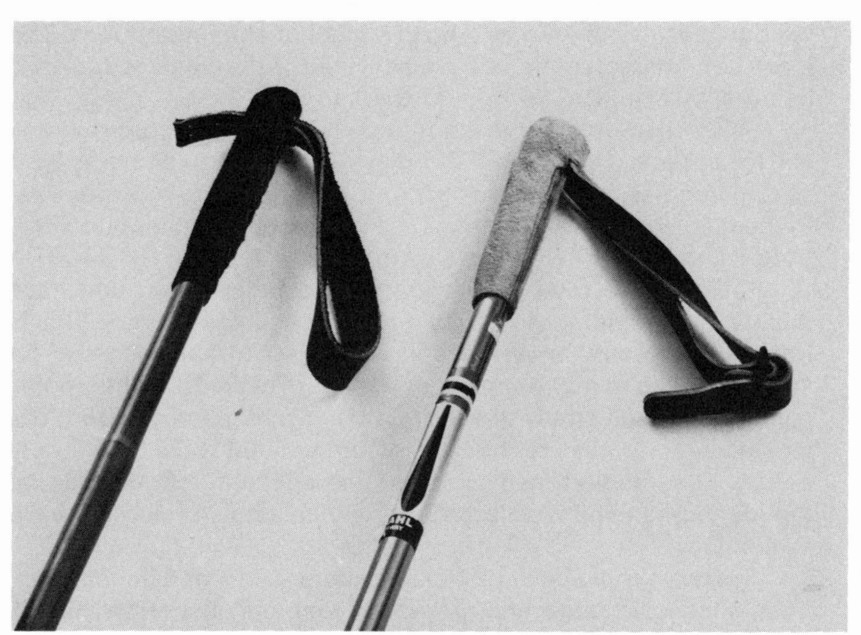

Top: *Pole handles have various types of adjustable straps.*

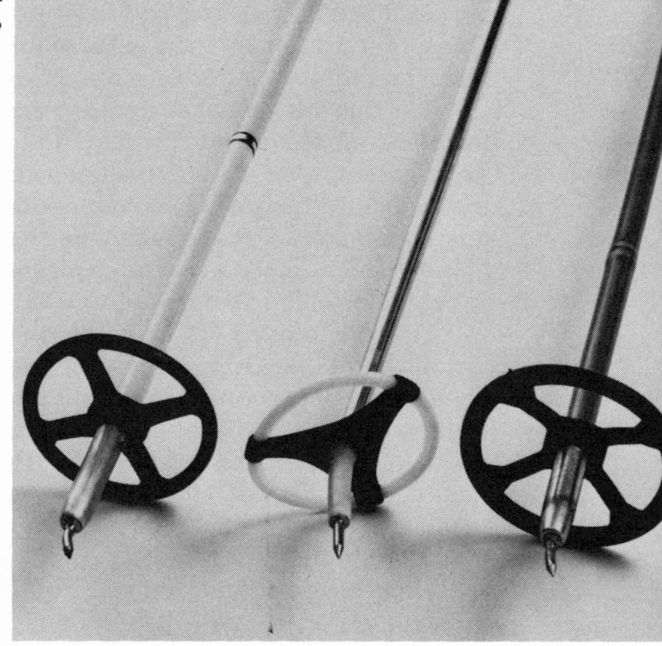

Bottom: Touring pole baskets are larger than those for cross-country racing.

hollow fiberglass tubes, and hollow steel or aluminum tubes. The ideal flex characteristic is best achieved if the shaft is tapered, being smaller at the tip than at the handle.

The tonkin pole is the traditional Nordic touring pole and is still the cheapest available. Fiberglass and metal poles are as light as tonkin poles, and far stronger, but are usually more expensive. In the last two Winter Olympics, fiberglass and metal poles were used by the majority of cross-country racers.

Poles for ski mountaineering should be stronger and have thicker shafts than those for light touring or cross-country. This is because ski-mountaineering poles must stand hard use and be strong enough to make emergency shelters or sleds. Lighter poles cannot stand the stress of such use. Thin-wall metal or fiberglass cross-country poles are thus not recommended for ski mountaineering. The simple tonkin pole has the advantage that it can be taped if broken and thus is the best choice if no sturdier poles are available.

Baskets should be light, flexible about the shaft, but not loose. They should be large enough not to sink into the snow. Cross-country racing poles, which are used on hard-packed tracks, have basket diameters up to about 3½ inches, while general-touring poles, which often are used in loose unpacked snow, have basket diameters of 4¼ inches or more.

Pole tips are bent at an angle to the shaft so that they can grip better on hard snow and crust. The tips are bent forward at an angle so that they are approximately vertical when the pole is in the middle of the poling movement of the diagonal stride. Pole tips should be sharpened when they become dull. Children's pole tips are usually made of rounded plastic rods as a safety measure. These poles will not bite very well on harder snow surfaces.

Straps and grips are made of leather, leather and plastic, or leather and cork. Grip shapes vary as there are many different opinions as to just what the proper shape should be. Most cross-country racers prefer a tapered elliptical grip with a rounded knob on top. The knob keeps the pole from sliding between their fingers when the hand is relaxed at the end of the poling movement, allowing the pole to be brought forward held only between thumb and forefinger.

A touring pole is correct in length when the top of the grip fits snugly under the armpit when you are standing on a level floor wearing your ski boots, with the pole vertical, point down, at your side.

SKIS, BINDINGS, AND BOOTS MUST MATCH

The golden rule in selecting touring equipment is that the various pieces must match. Cross-country racing skis should be used with cross-country racing bindings and boots. Likewise, general-touring skis should be used with general-touring bindings and boots. This is because heavier general-touring boots and bindings might pull off or damage a cross-country racing ski, and cross-country boots and bindings are too light to give control for general-touring skis, and so on.

Binding width should match boot width. If boots fit too tightly into bindings, soles can be shaved or sanded down slightly. Loose fits can be compensated for by tapping binding ears in slightly with a hammer.

SKI CLOTHING

Touring clothing must be warm but must not restrict body movement.

Air is an excellent insulator and it doesn't weigh very much. Thus clothing or clothing layers that trap air insulate well. The most porous fabrics, which trap lots of air, should form the innermost layers. The next layer should be a tighter-weave fabric which will then trap the air nearer the body.

But the outer layer should not be airtight or restrict air circulation completely. Complete restriction of circulation will result in

Correct clothing insulates. Layers near body trap air, and outer layers protect against wind.

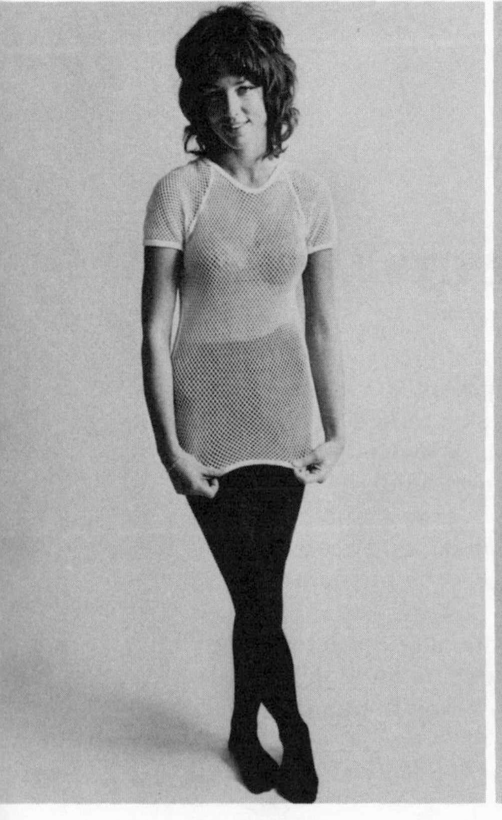

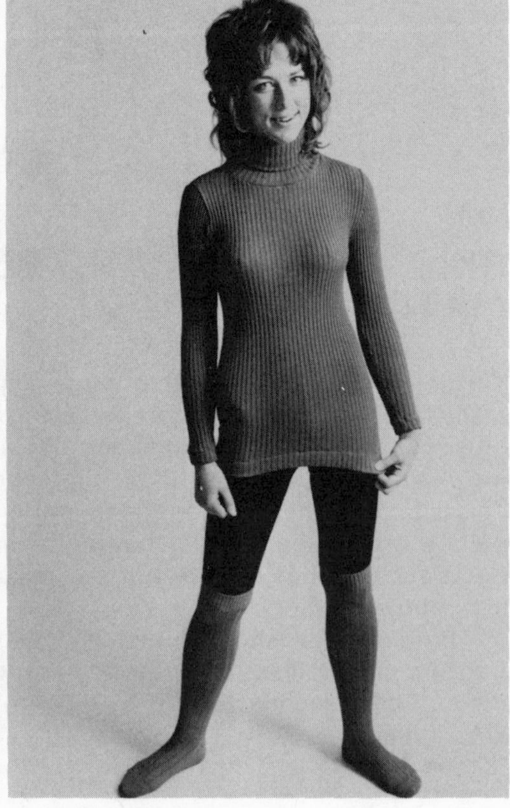

condensation of body perspiration, which will make clothing damp and clammy and heavy. Outer garments of tightly woven fabrics should have ventilating holes or openings on the upper back and under the arms plus a neck opening that can be regulated.

The innermost "air-filled" layers should be of materials that don't lose their insulating ability when wet. Wool and woollike synthetics are preferable to cotton. Fish-net shirts and long johns absorb very little moisture and trap a lot of air.

The basic insulating principles apply also to feet and hands.

Aside from these basic physical principles, one should dress according to weather, length of tour, physical condition, and in-

tended speed of tour. Thus a touring skier moving at a leisurely pace usually should wear tighter-weave garments than a cross-country racer who will sweat while running his event. Racers, in fact, usually have trouble keeping cool enough even though the air temperature may be well below freezing.

Stretch nylon is one of the most popular fabrics for ski-touring clothing. It allows a maximum of body movement freedom while providing just the right amount of insulation to both trap air and breathe. It doesn't tend to absorb water and thus won't increase much in weight because of absorbed perspiration or melted snow. But it isn't tight enough for use as outer clothing for wind protection. Nylon poplin or duck shell parkas and wind pants are recommended for extended tours.

Headgear

Knitted caps are the most popular for ski touring. Light-touring skiers and racers often add a knitted ear band or earmuffs for extra warmth. General-touring skiers and ski mountaineers should use a parka hood as extra protection.

Hands

Touring skiers can use a variety of gloves and mittens according to personal taste and needs. In general, the type of item selected depends on temperature. When air temperature is above freezing, you can use thin deerskin or perforated pigskin gloves; ordinary work gloves are fine and many racers have found that handball gloves work well. Or you may go barehanded if you prefer. Below freezing, down to about 25 degrees F., you can use the same type of gloves as for above freezing. But below 25 degrees, it's best to use some sort of wool or wool-leather mittens.

General-touring skiers should choose mittens which can be put on in layers. For instance, a pair of wool mittens which fit into leather or nylon shells are well suited to a range of temperatures.

Feet

Knee socks are the best bet for ski touring. Some skiers suffer more from cold feet than others, and should buy their boots large enough to allow room for two pairs of socks.

COLD-WEATHER DANGER

The Norwegian Red Cross has published the following hints for combating freezing and frost bite.

EARS Turn the affected ear to the lee (away from the direction) of the wind, and bend your head forward while the ear thaws. Hold a warm palm against the ear if possible. Avoid all movement of the ear during and after treatment.

NOSE Avoid movement during and after treatment. Stand with your back to the wind and bend your head forward. Keep your nose covered with a scarf or other garment, but not one that also covers your mouth.

CHEEKS Prevention: Saturate skin with clean, waterless salve prior to the tour. If affected, cover cheeks with scarf, bend head forward to lee of wind.

HANDS Prevention: Move vigorously, large swinging movements in circles or slapping opposite sides of body. First aid: Thaw under armpits. Change to dry mittens.

ABDOMEN Soft scarf inside knickers. A layer of newspaper, torn to fit crotch and placed between underwear and ski pants, insulates well. When skiing against the wind in an emergency, place a layer of newspaper under wind garments from your thighs up to your chest. Racers should use a pair of wind-tight trunks outside their long johns.

FEET Prevention: Move vigorously. Move feet with boots off. Change to dry socks. First aid: Thaw with no motion, warm against chest of another skier.

GENERAL FIRST AID A frozen part should be thawed WITHOUT MASSAGE OR MOVEMENT OF SKIN OR UNDERLYING BODY PART. The best source of warmth is the first aider's or the patient's own body warmth. In other words:

SKIN AGAINST SKIN

4

Waxing and Care of Skis

4

Waxing and Care of Skis

The gliding of skis and sled runners on types of snow is an extremely difficult subject. . . .
Fridtjof Nansen, 1930

More than forty years have passed since polar explorer Nansen wrote that classic introduction to an article on the gliding of skis on snow. Today's waxes and waxing equipment eliminate most of the problems of Nansen's time, but nobody can really say that they understand the science of waxing. The combination of grip and glide for touring still seems more of an art than a science. This chapter doesn't present the difficulties of waxing. It does present the basic principles and rules that make waxing easy. Start with the simple "learn to walk before you run," and waxing for ski touring and racing will be easy.

A LITTLE THEORY

It is difficult to explain why a waxed ski both grips and glides, chiefly because snow is what is known in scientific language as "visco elastic." That is, it sometimes acts like a viscous fluid such as motor oil and grease, sometimes like a flexible solid such as rubber, and sometimes like a semisolid that behaves like "silly-putty." The snow crystal type, density, and temperature determine which of these properties are present. They also determine the way the snow reacts to pressure, as applied by a weighted and/or gliding ski. Snow can rebound like rubber, flow like grease, shatter like lump sugar, or react in a combination of these ways. A microscopic look at both snow and wax will explain just how wax can both grip and glide on such stubborn stuff as snow.

A microscopic view of snow shows many irregularities: particles of different size, spacing, and stiffness arranged in many different directions. A corresponding microscopic picture of a waxed ski surface would show corresponding irregularities. The characteristics of the snow and the wax determine just how these irregularities mate with one another. When a ski is correctly waxed for touring or cross-country, the snow irregularities will dig into the wax irregularities just enough to give a motionless ski bite, or grip. But when the ski is in motion, the irregularities in the snow don't bite in; they even melt a bit to let the ski slide on a

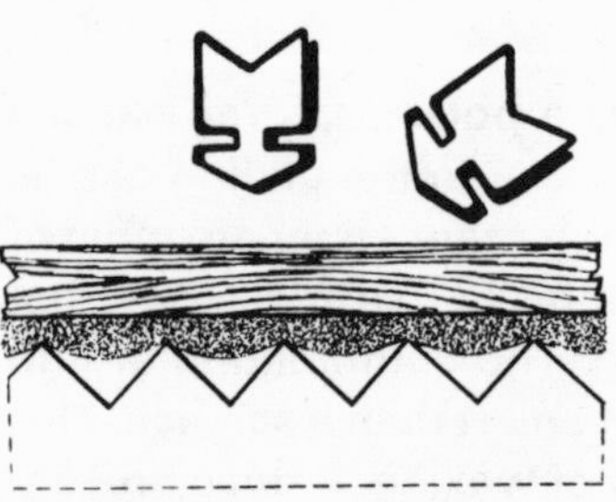

The friction under a ski at standstill is large, so it becomes a "platform" for the kick.

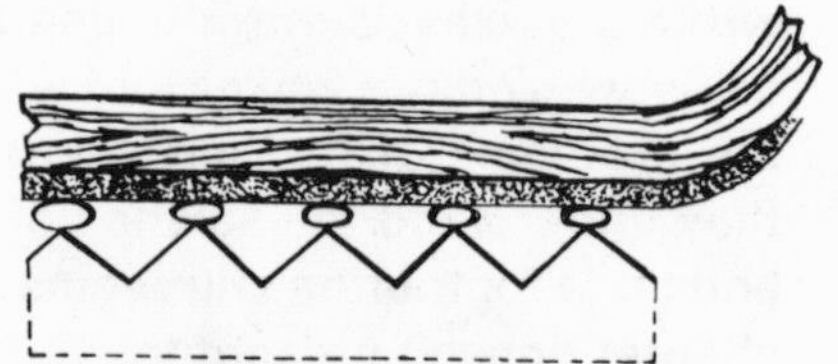

The friction under a gliding ski is less, partly because a microscopic water layer on the snow particles "lubricates" for low friction.

microscopic water layer. Thus wax can both grip and glide. A correctly waxed ski will glide as long as it is in motion. When gliding stops, it must be unweighted before it can glide again. A scientist would say that the coefficient of static (motionless) friction was greater than the coefficient of dynamic (in motion) friction. A touring skier would say the same thing: Standstill friction is greater than gliding friction.

This is the ideal. A ski can be waxed incorrectly in two ways: "too hard" and "too soft." If the wax is too hard for the snow involved, the ski will only slip and glide, it won't bite. If the wax is too soft for the snow involved, the snow irregularities can penetrate deep into the wax and stay there; the ski will grip and not glide and then will collect snow and ice up. So the major job in waxing is *first to judge the snow type and then select the correct wax.*

It's the difference between standstill friction and gliding friction that allows a ski to both grip and glide. This means that sometimes an unwaxed wood-based ski can both grip and glide. But were the same ski waxed correctly, it would have a better grip and a better glide. Waxing increases the difference between standstill friction and gliding friction, which is the real explanation of how wax works. In addition, wax protects a ski against moisture and wear. A good skier doesn't wear out his skis, he wears out his wax.

MAIN TYPES OF WAX

Base Preparation

Wood ski bottoms must be protected, or waterproofed. Wood absorbs water, water can freeze, and wax will not hold on wet or icy skis. There are two types of base preparation: impregnating compounds and tars. They come in a variety of cans, bottles, and spray containers.

From left to right: Impregnating, air-dry tar in brush-on and spray-on varieties, warm-in tar, and base waxes

Base preparation should be done whenever bare wood shows on a ski sole. Skis with synthetic bases or plastic-resin-wood bases need no base preparation.

Base Wax

Base waxes are durable binders used under final waxes for hard, icy conditions. There are three types: hard base wax for use under hard waxes, base klister for use under klisters, and universal base for use under all final waxes. Base waxes come in a variety of containers. Hard base waxes usually come in round foil cans about 1 ½ to 2 inches in diameter and 2 inches long. Base klisters usually come in tubes similar to toothpaste tubes. Universal base waxes usually come in foil cans or aerosol-spray containers.

Final Wax

"Hard wax" is used on dry snow. It usually comes in round foil cans about 1 ½ inches in diameter and about 2 inches long. The cans have either a thin foil wall which can be peeled off in strips to expose more wax, or with open ends allowing the wax to be pushed up as it is used.

"Klister-wax" is used on snow at freezing temperatures. It usually comes in the same type of cans as does hard wax.

"Klister" is used on wet snow and on icy tracks. It usually comes in tubes similar to toothpaste tubes.

Recently, several manufacturers have marketed final waxes in aerosol-spray cans.

HOW TO DO IT

Cleaning

Skilled touring skiers and cross-country racers prefer a scraper or a scraper and a waxing torch to clean skis. New wood skis sometimes have a protective base coat that must be removed before they are used. Check when buying new skis to see if they have this type of coating. If so, their bases should be scraped flat and smooth, with the final smoothing being done with sandpaper or

Top: Removing wax with a scraper

Bottom left: Removing klister with a ski scraper

Bottom right: Scraping with a carpenter's scraper

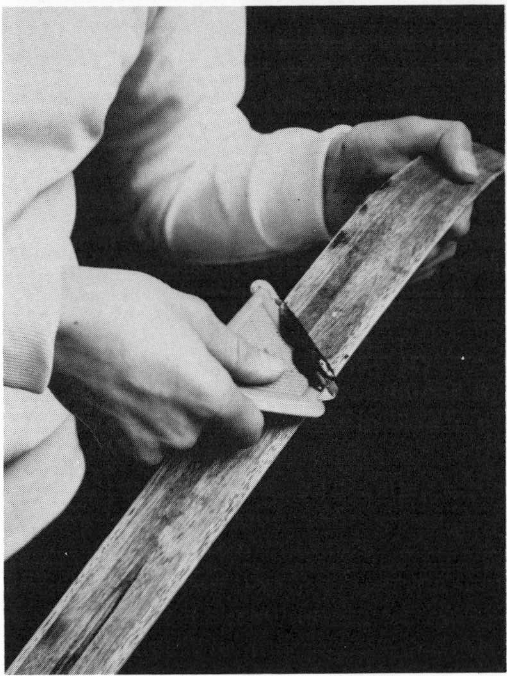

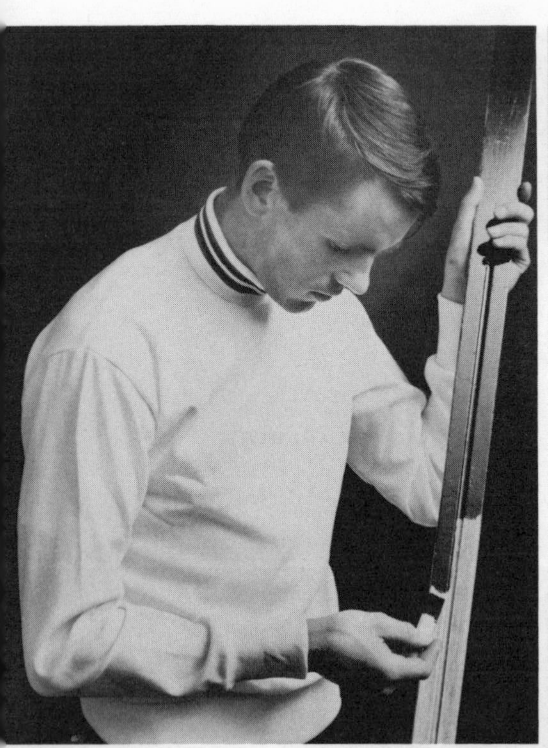

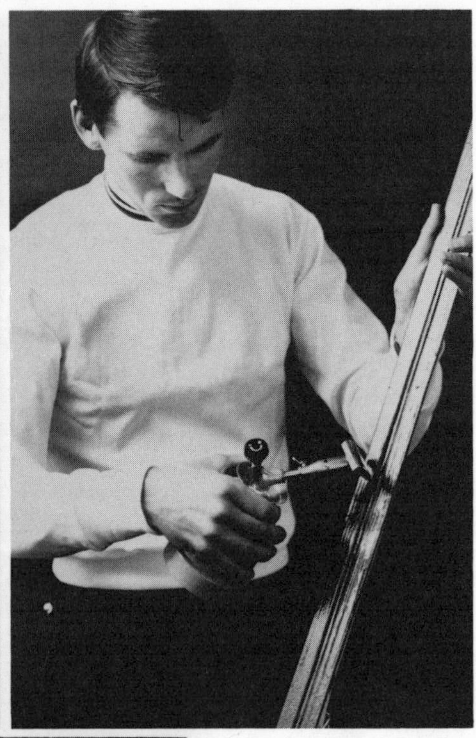

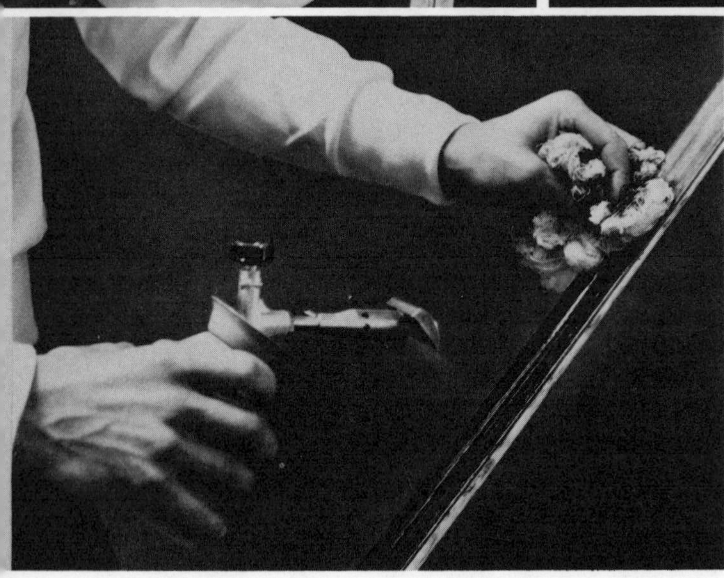

Top left: Tar brushed on

Top right: warmed in

Bottom left: and dried

steel wool. Skis with synthetic bases or epoxy-wood bases need not be sanded before use.

Greaseless cleaning fluids such as mineral turpentine, white gas, or cleaning fluids containing trichloroethylene can be used to remove wax. CAUTION: USE THESE CLEANING FLUIDS ONLY IN THE OPEN AS THEY ARE EITHER FLAMMABLE OR TOXIC OR BOTH.

Nonflammable wax-removing pastes and sprays are available. They are simply applied and then wiped off to remove wax.

Base preparation (wood bases only)

Impregnating compounds can be brushed or sprayed on, covering the entire ski sole. Most compounds dry in 8 to 12 hours.

Tar diluted in a thinner can be brushed or sprayed on and will air-dry. Thicker tar compounds must be warmed into the wood. Serious touring skiers and cross-country racers prefer the warm-in method as it gives the best base for waxing and gives maximum ski protection. Tar is first applied evenly over the entire ski sole, and then warmed with a waxing torch until it begins to bubble and smoke slightly. Then the excess is removed with a rag. The waxing torch should be moved continually to avoid burning the ski. The result should be a completely dry, chocolate-brown base. Warming ski bases can increase camber. If this happens, tie the skis together at the middle and warm their top sides gently immediately after tarring, and then let them stand a day.

Base Wax

If needed, base wax is best applied with a waxing torch or waxing iron, and then smoothed out with a waxing cork.

Choosing and Using Wax

Sometimes old wax must be removed before new wax is applied. Klister should be removed at the end of every tour. Waxing is easiest indoors.

The *only* problem in choosing the right wax is judging the snow conditions correctly. The type of snow, size of particle, and moisture content determine its characteristics. The moisture in snow is determined by the snow and air temperatures, by humidity in the air, and by precipitation. At temperatures below freezing, snow temperature is usually the same as still-air temperature. At temperatures above freezing, snow temperature can be the same as or below still-air temperature. So you can trust a wall thermometer only for subfreezing temperatures.

For waxing, snow is classified as new snow, old fine-grained snow, and snow with modified crystals such as corn, ice, and crust. In each case it can be dry, wet, or in the transition between dry and wet. These classifications are used in the waxing table.

Test snow with a gloved hand. Squeeze a handful tight and then open your hand. If the snow blows away, it's dry. If it forms a tight snowball, then it's wet. If it breaks up into small clumps, it's in the transition between wet and dry.

The waxing table on pages 88, 90–91 lists the waxes from the nine manufacturers marketing a full line in the United States. The table is only a guide and is not precise for all products. The temperature ranges listed are averages of those given by the different manufacturers. Follow the individual manufacturer's instructions on the wax cans or tubes before you wax.

Hard wax is crayoned on evenly and rubbed out to a gloss with a waxing cork. If you have no cork, you can rub out hard wax with the edge or bottom of the wax can. Hard wax can be made harder (work at lower temperatures) and more durable if it is warmed on with a waxing iron. Warmed-on wax should also be corked out.

Klister-wax, as its name implies, is something between klister and wax. It comes in the same sort of cans as does hard wax and should be applied in the same way. It can be spread evenly with a scraper or rubbed out with the palm of your hand. Don't use a waxing cork as the cork particles will stick to the tacky surface and ruin the wax characteristics. Klister-wax can also be warmed on with a waxing iron.

Klister is a thick, tacky fluid. Klister hardens when cold, so it should always be applied warm. It should be spread out with a scraper or spreader, or rubbed out with the palm of your hand. Klister should not be corked out.

It's difficult if not impossible to get wax to hold on a wet ski. Skis should be dried before waxing. Hard wax won't hold on softer wax (wax for "warmer" or "older" snow), nor will klister hold on hard wax or klister-wax. Soft wax should be removed before applying harder wax, and hard wax or klister-wax should be removed before applying klister.

Wax the entire bottom of a ski, always in thin layers, never in one thick layer. Applying more layers to the area of the ski under the binding and forward and back for a total length of about a third of the ski will increase wax bite or "kick." It makes no difference in which direction you apply or rub out wax.

Newly waxed skis should be allowed to cool to outside temperature before being used. Avoid placing them directly in snow, as snow will adhere to warmer wax and the skis will then ice up. Newly waxed skis often must be skied on a little before they bite and glide as they should; 5 to 10 minutes of skiing is usually enough.

Left: Hard wax is "crayoned on" evenly.
Right: Klister is best applied in strips.

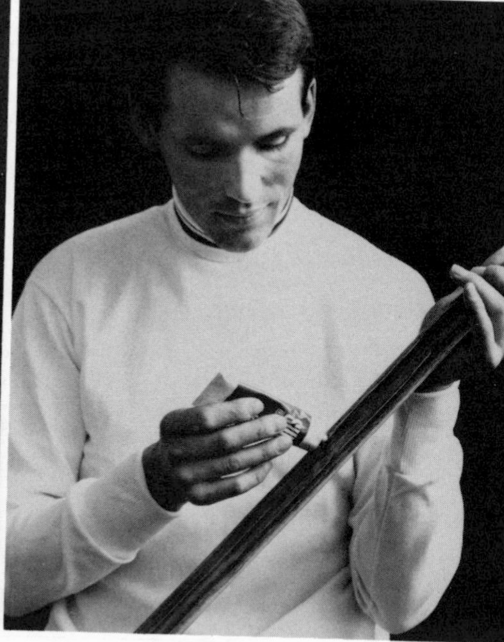

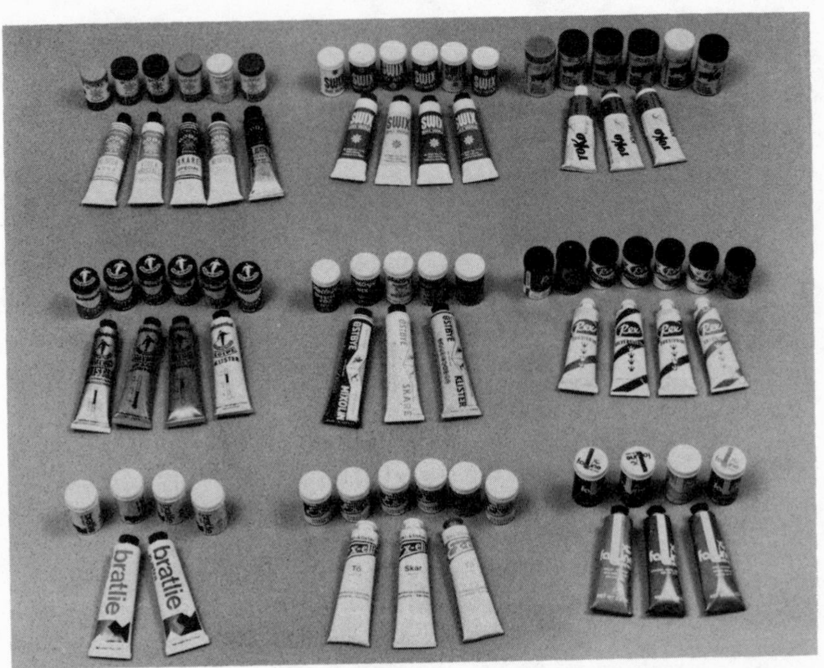

Waxes of nine manufacturers listed in Table 2

Table 1: BASE TREATMENT

IMPREG-NATING COMPOUNDS	TAR PREPARATIONS			BASE WAXES
	Air Dry		Warm-in	
	Brush-on	Spray		
Bergendahl	Bergendahl	Bratlie Holmenkol	Bratlie Holmenkol	Östbye Mixolin Wax
Östbye Mixol	Karhu	Karhu	Karhu	Rex Grundvalla Bratlie Spray
	Rex	Östbye	Lasse Back	Rode Chola Klister
	Suolahden	Petälä	Rode	Rode Nera
	Swix	Swix	Suolahden	Swix Grundvalla
	Toko	Toko	Swix	Swix Spray for Synthetic Base Skis
			Tento 50	Toko Grundvalla

TEN RULES FOR SUCCESSFUL WAXING

1 CHECK snow conditions before you wax. Note:
Temperature
Moisture in the air (humidity, fog, rain, snow, clear etc.)
Test the snow—gloved hand!

2 READ the manufacturer's directions on the can or tube before you wax—they are usually right.

3 APPLY wax evenly and rub it out well.

4 USE SEVERAL THIN LAYERS: the more layers, the better the kick, but too many layers reduce glide.

5 A SOFTER WAX grips better than a hard wax. But a softer wax can reduce glide.

6 A HARD WAX is a good base for a softer wax, but not vice versa.

7 EXPERIMENT with each wax you use until you know it well. When in doubt, use different numbers of layers of waxes you know well instead of changing to waxes you don't know.

8 PICK one manufacturer's set of waxes and learn their characteristics as they suit your skiing and the snow conditions and altitude where you normally ski.

9 LEARN CENTIGRADE temperatures if you can. They're handy for waxing: plus means wet snow, minus means dry snow, and zero means the borderline.

10 KEEP OUT MOISTURE: Skis that have absorbed moisture won't hold wax well, and may warp, lose their camber, or break more easily than they would if base-treated properly.

Simplified Waxing

The waxing table is a guide to selecting the waxes now available to match all snow conditions precisely. It may seem to indicate that an enormous array of waxes is necessary for touring. This is far from true; if you're not a cross-country racer interested in

Table 2: Waxes for All Conditions

Snow Type and Characteristics		Temperatures Usually in the Range		Bratlie NORWAY	Ex-Elit SWEDEN	Fall-Lin U.S.A
		°C.	°F.			
Falling and New Snow	Extremely dry (falling powder)	−3° and below	18° and below	Green	Cold Special (Black)	Green
	Very dry (powdery: blows easily)	−5° and below	21° and below	Green	Green	Green
	Dry (blows with difficulty)	0° to −5°	23° to 32°	Blue	Blue	Blue
	Transition borderline (clumps in gloved hand)	−1° to +1°	30° to 34°	Violet	Violet/ Red	Purple
	Mushy (rolling snowballs dig in)	0° to +3°	32° to 37°	Red	Yellow	Yellow
	Wet (hand soaking wet after squeezing)	+2° to +6°	35° to 42°	Red Klister	Tö Kristal Klister	Red Klister
Settled Snow	Very dry (small crystals will blow)	−12° and below	10° and below	Green	Cold Special/ Green	Green
	Dry (small crystals will form snowballs)	−1° to −10°	14° to 30°	Blue	Blue	Blue
	Transition borderline (large crystals, corns, or clumps)	−1° to +1°	30° to 34°	Violet	Violet/ Red	Purple
	Mushy (hand wet after squeezing	0° to +3°	32° to 37°	Red/ Red Klister	Red/Tö Kristal Klister	Red Klist Purple Kl
	Wet (slushy)	+2° to +6°	35° to 42°	Red Klister	Tö Kristal Klister	Red Klist
Metamorphosized Snow ("Skare": Ice, Crust; Pack, Heavy Corn, Slush)	"Skare"—dry, hard, ice, crust, etc.	−5° and below	21° and below	Blue Klister	Skar Kristal Klister	Blue Klist
	Crusty but softer to mushy and wet	−6° to +1°	22° to 34°	Blue and Red Klisters mixed	Skar Kristal and Tö Kristal Klisters mixed	Purple Kl
	Wet slush	0° to +6°	32° to 42°	Red Klister	Tö med Tjära Klister	Red Klist

NOTE: Klisters are in tubes, and waxes are in cans. Listing under a manufacturer is only a g

olmenkol ERMANY	Östbye NORWAY	Rex FINLAND	Rode ITALY	Swix NORWAY	Toko SWITZERLAND
ve	Green Mix	Special 8571/ Light Green	Light Green	Special Green	Olive
een	Blue Mix	Green	Green	Green	Green
e	Blue Mix	Blue	Blue	Blue/ Extra Blue	Blue
let	Medium/ Klistervox	Violet	Violet	Extra Blue/ Violet	Red
d	Klistervox	Yellow	Yellow	Yellow	Yellow
ow/ ow ter	"Klister"	Red Klister	Red Klister	Yellow Klister	Yellow/ Red Klister
ve/ een	Green Mix	Light Green/ Green	Light Green/ Green	Special Green/ Green	Olive/ Green
e	Blue Mix	Blue	Blue	Blue/ Extra Blue	Blue
let	Medium/ Mixolin Klister	Violet/ Violet Klister	Violet/ Violet Klister	Extra Blue/ Violet	Violet
/ ow	Klistervox/ Mixolin Klister	Red/ Red Klister	Red/ Red Klister	Red/ Violet Klister	Yellow
ow ter	"Klister"	Red Klister	Silver Klister/ Red Klister	Red Klister	Red Klister/ Violet Klister
e ter	Mixolinvox/ Skare Klister	Blue Klister	Blue Klister/ Red Klister	Blue Klister	Blue Klister
e Klister/ er Klister	Mixolinvox/ Mixolin Klister	Violet Klister	Violet Klister	Violet Klister	Violet Klister
er Klister/ Klister	"Klister"	Silver Klister and Red Klister mixed	Silver Klister/ Black Klister	Red Klister	Red Klister

d directions before waxing.

skiing every mile as fast as possible, waxing can be vastly simplified. A single wax for dry snow, one for wet snow, and one for transition snow will cover most ski-touring needs. Many manufacturers offer a three-wax ski-touring kit for just this purpose. With the addition of one klister, the touring skier has wax to meet all ski-touring snow conditions.

Problems

Transition-snow conditions and changing snow conditions are the real tests of waxing ability. The most difficult of transition conditions is when new dry snow falls and then slowly gets wet when in contact with the existing warmer snow surface. The best way to tackle transition waxing problems is to start with a layer of hard wax and then apply more layers of the same wax if the skis don't bite. If these several layers don't give bite, add a layer of softer wax in the middle of the ski.

Sometimes moisture works under wax at transition temperatures and causes skis to collect snow and ice up. The best remedy is to keep moving and keep your skis in contact with the snow: Don't lift them up from the snow at all.

Surface water on frozen lakes poses one of the most serious ski-icing problems for any type of skis, be they waxed skis or "waxless" skis. Even at temperatures considerably below freezing, a few inches of snow are enough to insulate the ice surface so that it can be just at or even a little above freezing. The top surface of the ice can melt slightly, or temperature variations can "pump" lake water up onto the ice where it will remain unfrozen because it is insulated by the snow above. A skier may cut tracks in the cold snow that go all the way down to this water layer. Cold skis in contact with water will ice up almost immediately. Double pole with equally weighted skis through surface water stretches to minimize icing, but always take along a scraper if your tour is to go over frozen lakes.

Different snow conditions require different types of wax, so waxing for changing conditions is perhaps the most difficult of waxing problems. A touring skier can stop and relax, but a racer usually cannot. The only solution on waxing for changing conditions is to learn the types of changes that occur where you ski and wax accordingly.

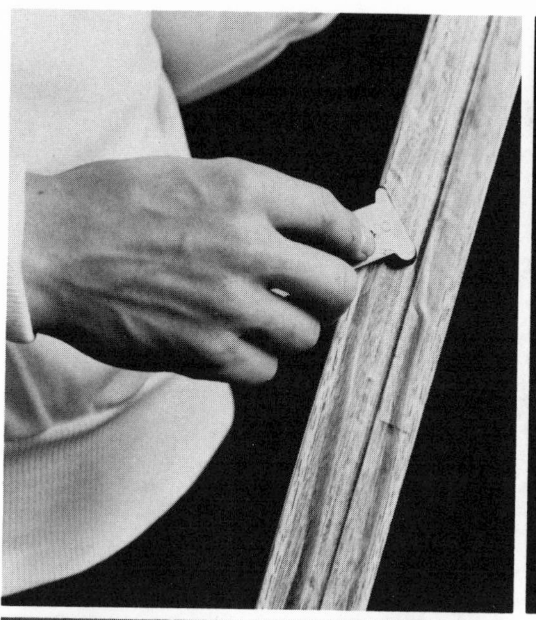

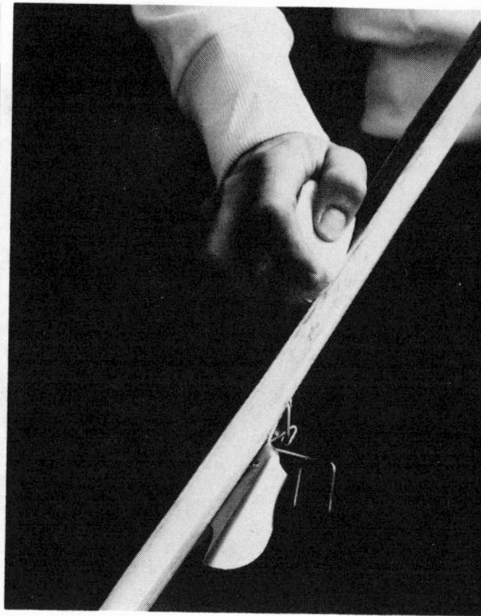

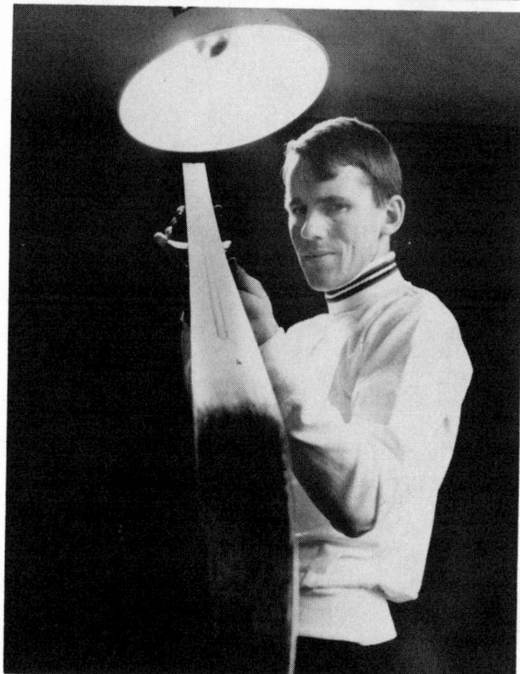

Top left: Klister is easily spread out with a scraper or a spreader.

Top right: Hard wax is best rubbed out and polished with a waxing cork.

Bottom: A well-waxed ski should shine, but not necessarily be mirror-smooth.

Quick-application sprays and pastes

Sprays and Pastes

Several manufacturers make both hard waxes and klisters dissolved in thinners so they can be sprayed on from aerosol cans or applied as pastes to make wax application easier. The thinners must be given time to dry—usually 15 minutes or so.

To date, the hard-wax sprays and pastes are not as durable as the ordinary wax in cans, but spray klisters are satisfactory. Spray klisters on synthetic-base skis are just as durable as klister applied from the tube.

SOME SECRETS OF WAXING FOR CROSS-COUNTRY RACING

Experienced cross-country racers often seem to treat and wax their skis in direct opposition to usual practice. There are reasons for what they do, and it isn't all black magic.

Base Preparation

Modern cross-country racing skis are light, thin, and not very strong. Experienced racers are careful with torches when warming in tar, because excessive heat will bulge and bow thin tips and tails. Tar is of little use if all the wax added later rubs off in the middle of a race. Thus cross-country racers wax in layers, with the first layer being the toughest and most durable wax for the conditions involved.

Waterproofing ski bases is a must for all, racers included. But often racers scrape their skis almost to bare wood just after having warmed in tar—and the drier the snow conditions, the more scraping. But they're still observing the basic rule; they follow the scraping immediately by waxing with base wax or a warmed-in layer of the day's wax followed by several thin layers of wax. They want to keep the tar from working its way through the wax to slow the skis. Sometimes racers even scrape their skis to bare wood before applying wax for races in cold, dry snow conditions. In any event, they never let scraped skis stand around to absorb moisture—which would cause the skis to warp or lose their camber.

Top: Larger wax kits hold all waxing needs.

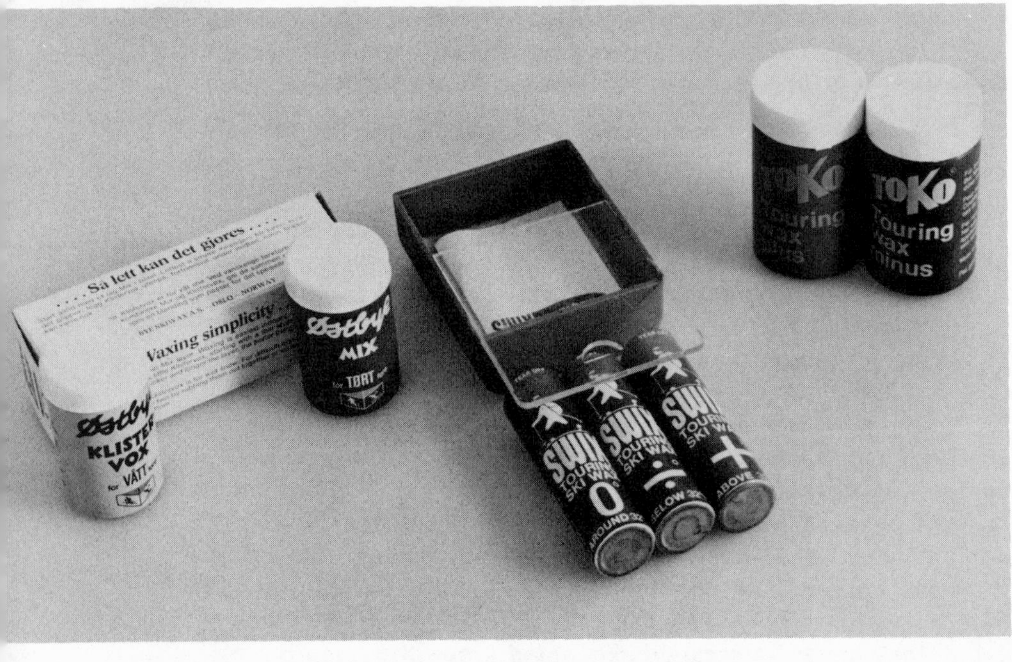

Bottom: Smaller kits meet all touring needs.

They wax immediately, being careful to cover every bit of bare wood with several well-rubbed-out layers of wax. This waterproofs the skis. Any small area of the ski bottom that has no wax will ice up—a well-rubbed-out dry snow wax will seldom ice up.

Choice of and Application of the Day's Wax

Base wax is intended for hard, dry conditions, and knowledgeable racers use it only when they fear a really abrasive track that will wear wax quickly. Base wax tends to "draw" on fine snow, making kicks difficult and slowing glides. A racer may risk running on bare skis toward the end of a race, rather than risk the braking effect of base wax.

Hard wax gives a better glide than soft wax, a rule that is really true only over intervals for each type of wax. A hard racing wax that results in hopelessly slippery skis will also result in a poor glide—it "draws" the skis to the snow. Experienced racers then try to find the wax that gives just the right grip or "kick"—it will be the wax that will give the best glide, no matter whether it is a klister or a hard wax.

Soft waxes grip better than hard waxes. This is true for the temperatures for which they should be used, but is false for subfreezing temperatures. Soft waxes freeze at low temperatures; icing makes skis slippery—they slip backward and won't glide forward.

Rubbing out wax to an even and smooth layer is the general rule. But sometimes snow in racing tracks is tightly packed and so smooth that a smooth wax surface "draws." It is then better to leave the last wax layer a bit uneven.

A wax warmed into a ski becomes harder, or more like a "colder" wax (i.e., a wax suitable for colder snow), and is more durable than a wax that has simply been rubbed on. But a wax that has been warmed too much becomes brittle, and can crack and flake off. All warmed-on wax should be polished with a cork before being used.

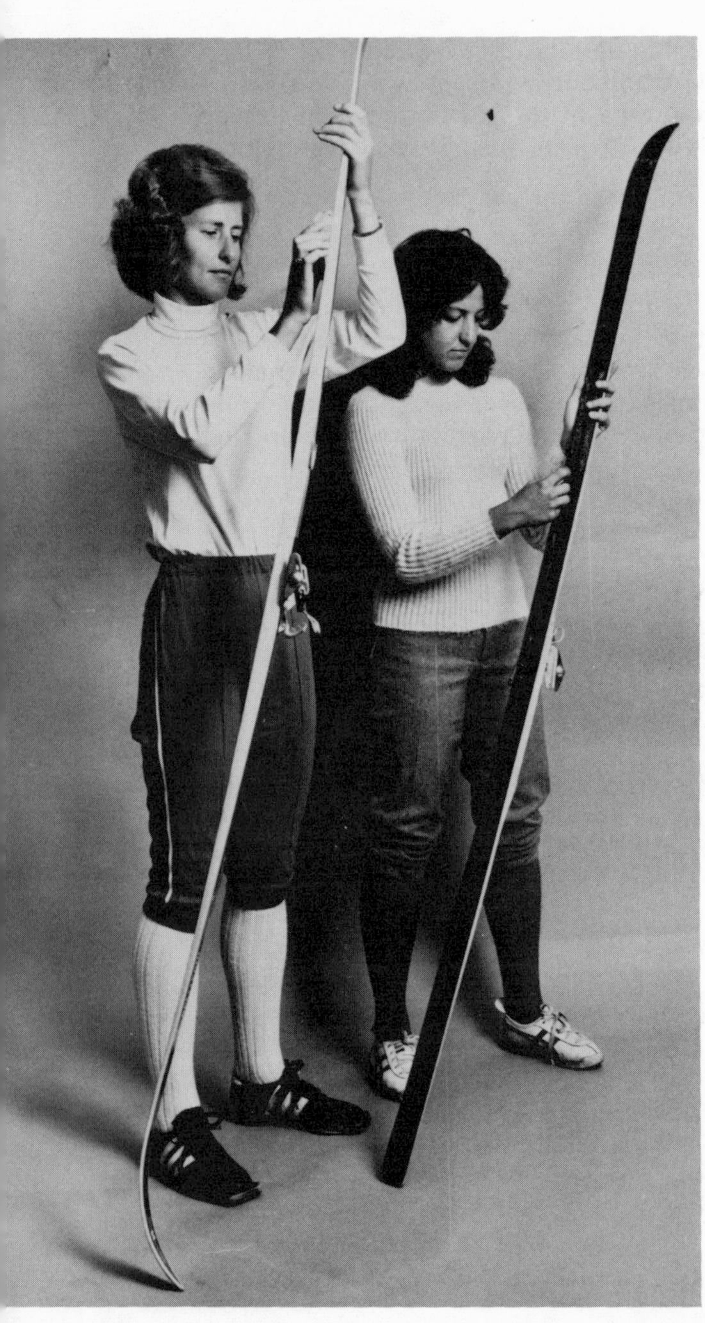

Waxing's for all. . . .

WAXING AIDS

Ski scrapers and waxing corks are indispensable. They do a faster, more effective job, as well as save wear and tear on hands and fingernails. Many types are available, both separate and as combined scraper-corks. Corks, as the name implies, were once made from natural cork. Synthetic corks are now more common than natural cork. Most synthetic corks are made of expanded plastics (plastics blown full of air bubbles).

Waxing irons are small and light and several types are available. One handy type uses fuel tablets to heat the hollow aluminum block of the iron.

A pocket waxing thermometer helps judge snow conditions.

Waxing torches are useful for warming in base preparations, removing old wax and klisters, drying wet skis before waxing, or for heating a waxing iron quickly. Waxing torches can be classified as being either liquid- or gas-fueled.

Liquid-fueled torches: Several models of pump-pressurizing kerosene torches and self-pressurizing gasoline torches are available. They are inexpensive and their fuels are available almost anywhere. Despite this, gas torches have all but replaced liquid-fuel torches because they are convenient to use and easy to light and because the gases used as fuels deliver about 10 percent more heat for their weight than do gasoline or kerosene.

Gas torches are available using either refillable liquid propane cylinders or disposable liquid butane cartridges. The propane cylinders are far heavier than the butane cartridges for the same amount of gas, but have the advantage that propane burns well down to −22 degrees F. while butane "freezes" at +31 degrees F.* The choice between the two types then depends on fuel avail-

---

*Most butane cartridges actually freeze at a slightly lower temperature because the butane is not pure but contains small amounts of propane (freezes at −44° F.) and isobutane (freezes at +10° F.) impurities. The reason why liquid propane is not

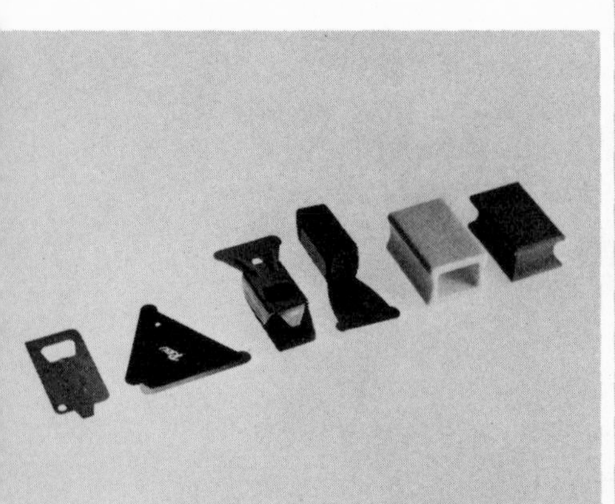

Top left: Corks and scrapers, the basic waxing tools
Top right: Waxing irons and waxing thermometers, advanced tools
Bottom: Smaller butane-cartridge torches and a larger propane tank torch

ability and on use; for a torch to be carried on tours it is a choice of a heavy propane torch which always works in cold weather or a lighter butane torch which must be warmed inside clothing or by hand in subfreezing weather.

Stand in the lee of the wind whenever using a torch outdoors. In subfreezing weather, allow butane cartridge torches to run a couple of minutes after they are lit and try to keep the tank and valve stem vertical as much as possible during use. When using waxing-iron attachments to torches, regulate the flame to keep the iron from getting so warm that it vaporizes the wax. Turn off the flame for a while if the iron gets too hot.

Special wax-dissolving hand cleaners and most mechanic's waterless hand cleaners will remove wax from hands or clothing. Ordinary vaseline is a good solvent for klisters. These types of cleaners should not be used on skis, as they will penetrate the surface and make future waxing difficult. Some wax manufacturers make special cleaning compounds for skis that are simply squeezed on from a tube or sprayed on from an aerosol can and then wiped off to remove wax.

STORING SKIS

Skis must be cleaned before being stored for any length of time, because wax left on skis hardens and is difficult to remove. Wood-based skis must also be base-treated before being stored, because any bare wood will absorb moisture and soften the skis or ruin their camber. Scratches on the top and sides can be sealed by rubbing on a bit of paraffin wax. If skis are well prepared for storage, they will retain their camber no matter

---

available in disposable cartridges is that at room temperature (70° F.) it exerts a pressure of 124 pounds per square inch on its container, while liquid butane exerts a pressure of 32 pounds per square inch on its container—about the same pressure as in many automobile tires. At temperatures of 100° F. as might be encountered in transport and storage, butane pressure increases to 52.2 pounds per square inch. At the same temperature, propane pressure has increased to 187 pounds per square inch, which is more than enough to explode any known type of disposable container.

whether they are laid flat, stood on end, or tied or bound in any manner. They can simply be stood in a corner or in a closet.

Excessive camber can be reduced in storage by strapping a pair of skis together at their midpoints, and gently but thoroughly heating their top sides before storage.

Deficient camber is difficult to correct. Blocking skis, a common practice thirty years ago, will only distort the tips and tails of modern laminated skis. The best way to increase the camber of laminated-wood skis is to heat the skis thoroughly in the mid sections of their bases before storage.

The tips and tails of laminated skis can be altered by warming both top and bottom surfaces, and gently bending as required. Warped tails, often caused by moisture absorbed when skis stand in puddles of melted snow, can be corrected in the same manner.

A WAXING FABLE

Once there was a timid tourer who couldn't wax. But he wanted to learn, so he went to a ski shop that specialized in ski touring. There he found wax of all types and varieties, in cans, in tubes, and in spray cans. And he found things to put it on with, things to warm it, and things to take it off with. He was more confused than ever.

But the clerk was conscientious and helpful, and he knew a good customer when he saw one. So he told the timid tourer: "Just buy one can of dry-snow hard wax now, and you won't have so much to keep track of. When it's really cold, put on a thin layer. When it gets warmer and your skis start to slip instead of grip, put on a few more layers. Afterward, you can buy more wax and waxing aids as you need them."

The timid tourer was happy; maybe waxing wasn't so bad after all. Besides, he had walked out of the shop with a lot of change still in his pocket. A good deal. In the beginning, he did very well with that one can. He waxed with one or two thin layers when it was cold, and with many layers when it was warmer. He used the bottom of the can to rub out the wax.

Later he went back to the shop and bought a waxing cork. It was his second investment.

BLUE

klister
wax

KLISTER

And a little later he started to use two waxes: his old standby hard wax for below freezing and a klister-wax for above freezing. He had confidence in the old standby, but he had found that it couldn't be made to work for all conditions.

Then he went back to the shop again and bought a tube of klister, which he learned to use on crusty, icy, and wet snow.

A little later he bought a scraper because it was handy. He had been scraping ice off a ski with the edge of the shovel of the other ski, because once in a while he had misjudged the snow or run into changing conditions where his skis iced up. He even found the scraper better for removing old wax than the back edge of his hunting knife, which he had been using.

"Now all you need is a waxing torch for warming in wax when you're outdoors or to remove wax at anytime," his friend the clerk told him, "and then you've mastered the basics of waxing."

By then the timid tourer knew well how to use

He had a hand cleaner at home which worked like a charm on wax. And he didn't need to buy rags to use when removing wax with a torch.

"Well, let's start on a bit more advanced waxing," the clerk told him one day. "Now take one of the three main types of wax at a time, and learn how to use more of what's available."

The timid tourer carried on with gusto, but he was, as always, very careful. He read the instructions on every can and tube, and he didn't buy any wax before he knew well how to use those he already had.

Finally the timid tourer was no longer timid. His skis always glided as they should, and he had a good "kick." He never made a mistake with his wax. This drew attention; other skiers admired him. They couldn't understand why he always had good skis when they often struggled with slippery skis or with clods of snow glued to their ski bottoms.

After one tour, they all surrounded him. "You're a waxing wizard," one said, "you never miss. What about letting us in on your secret?" " 'Fraid not," replied the timid tourer who was no longer timid, "not if you mean that I should divulge some sort of secret right here and now. But I can help you get started, so you can teach yourselves how to wax. It's the simplest, and really the only way to learn the ins and outs of waxing. For instance, each one of you can go out and buy a single can of dry-snow hard wax, and when you get to know it well . . ."

5
Fitness and Training

5

Fitness and Training

Passive fitness, the mere absence of any illness, is a losing battle. Without activity, the body begins to deteriorate.
Kenneth H. Cooper, *Aerobics*

It's a beautiful Sunday in autumn in the woods near a town in the snow belt. A few couples are strolling along a logging road. Some hikers are coming back from one of the higher trails. Many families are out, just taking a Sunday walk.

Suddenly a powerfully built athlete comes running, running hard. He's huffing and puffing; sweat streams from his whole body. He's in training, they all say, he's training really hard.

Now here comes a gang of boys, all ten to twelve years old. They must be scouts, they've all got knapsacks on their backs, and their leader is a man old enough to be their grandfather. He remembers many such hikes. . . .

Now a slightly built girl trots up one of the trails, lithely jumping from stone to fallen log and onto the ground again. Most of the townspeople seem to know her. She's wearing shorts and a T-shirt from a southern vacation center. She stops, chats with a girl friend, and then jogs on again. But most of the people are just walking.

Who's exercising, who's training on this Sunday? Was it only the athlete who really had a rough time, who really "trained hard"? What about the boys on a long hike? And what about the girl? Everyone in town knew who she was; they had seen her name in the papers all last winter. And what about all the families who were "just walking?" They were moving, some of them a long way.

The answer is that all who were out in the woods that Sunday were training because: *Training is any physical activity that improves or maintains physical ability.*

But what do you get out of training, that is, physical training, as it should be called here? Must you train until it hurts to get any results? Hardly. Training doesn't have to be strenuous, hard, or unpleasant to produce results. You should *train fitness into, not out of, yourself.*

What is correct training? What is right for a touring skier and what is right for a cross-country ski racer?

Clearly few touring skiers need to train the way racers do, nor do they have the time or inclination to do so. On the other hand, cross-country racers, who compete in one of the most demanding events in athletics, must train as athletes; exercise as done by a touring skier would simply be inadequate for them.

So training is really a personal thing, suited to individual tastes and needs. With the definition that training is "any physical activity that improves or maintains physical ability," this chapter might equally well have been called "activity" or "recreation for skiing." But "training" is the correct term. It doesn't mean "getting in shape" or "hurting." It's the physical activity that you do naturally or do intentionally, and it should always be enjoyable.

TRAINING PRINCIPLES AND TRAINING PROGRAMS

The same general training principles apply for all; the well trained merely train longer, harder, and more often than the untrained. Therefore, in this chapter training will be called "cross-country training" and ski technique will be called "cross-country technique." The principles involved apply equally well to conditioning for recreational ski touring and to ski touring technique. The training program, or "fitness program" followed by any one skier depends on age, sex, personal needs, ability, and level of fitness.

Personal experience is the best guide to determining the amount and intensity of exercise in a training program, especially for the active athletic cross-country racer. Racers should make notes of their training, their races, and their physical tests. Touring skiers can simply make mental notes of how well they ski in any season in relation to what they did the autumn and summer before. These written or mental notes indicate the effectiveness of your personal training program.

DEMANDS

Exercise, in the physiological sense, is all muscle work—for instance, walking, running, rowing, cycling, skiing, chopping wood, sit-ups, push-ups.

Competitive cross-country skiing demands much from the entire person but it is very difficult to define precisely what sort of body work is involved. The effort the body expends varies from course to course, and varies within the same course. No one particular effort can be singled out, for length or intensity, and movement patterns and movement power vary according to the course's profile and snow conditions.

The sport requires endurance, muscular fitness, technique, and psychological strength. The major divisions of training for ski touring and cross-country racing develop the first three physical abilities.

Endurance

Endurance fitness enables prolonged work to be done without fatigue.

Cross-country races for senior men vary from 30 minutes to 3 hours or more in length. Races for boys and girls range from 10 to 30 minutes, and women's races last up to 40 minutes. Racers can rest on downhills, but the total time spent resting is small. Cross-country thus requires continuous work output. *Endurance fitness is the dominant requirement for cross-country racing and for ski touring.*

The level of endurance fitness, or work capacity, is less for a touring skier than for a racer, but both should regard endurance fitness as the major part of their overall fitness.

Muscular Fitness

Muscular fitness is the ability of the skeletal muscles to perform the movement required; these movements need *strength* and *resilience.*

Strength is the ability to lift, push, or pull against a resistance. Strength is the dominant component of muscular fitness. But muscular strength alone, as emphasized by body builders, *specifically does not* mean muscular fitness or overall physical fitness.

Resilience depends largely on muscle strength. Resilience for a cross-country skier defines many things, such as the ability to kick rapidly with each kick, and the ability to sprint up small hills.

Flexibility and Agility

Flexibility is a measure of maximum movement. For instance, how far can you bend forward when standing with knees straight; how far can you bend forward at the ankles when squatting; or how long a stride can you take walking uphill?

Agility is another way of expressing flexibility, but is more concerned with the aesthetic whole of a movement. Agility can be defined as the ability to use body flexibility in the most efficient manner.

Efficient and correct cross-country technique uses almost all the major muscle groups in the body. Thus, to be a good cross-country skier, one needs an all-around muscular tone and development. Lean efficiency rather than bulging muscles are the goal.

Cross-country racing is an event involving many changes in conditions and techniques. The force and duration of kick and poling movements vary continually according to the terrain inclination. Bending and stretching movements in ankle, knee, and hip joints vary according to track, terrain, and snow, and are repeated thousands of times during a race. These require agility and considerable endurance in the leg, arm, back, and frontal muscles.

Technique

"Good" cross-country technique is that which always employs the most appropriate movements for the circumstances. Diagonal striding and double poling, discussed in Chapter 2, are the most common movements in cross-country skiing. Good technique enables the skier to change between these movements and other similar strides as well as to modify each movement slightly to suit course and snow conditions. Course variations are not the same from race to race. Short or long, gentle or steep hills, flat stretches, bumps and dips, turns, gentle or steep downhills are found in most cross-country courses. The variations are infinite. Therefore cross-country technique requires "feel" and an ability to improvise and change. Rhythm is, of course, a vital part of technique, as is the ability to glide. An analysis of any one skiing style amounts to an analysis of the kick and the poling movements, which are really the most important parts of the cross-country strides.

Psychological Strength

Psychological strength is important in all competition. Racers should be able to tolerate defeat as well as enjoy winning, or they will not be able to enjoy competition.

Experience and mental alertness are the primary mental abilities useful to a cross-country racer.

Cross-country training takes lots of time. The major part of off-snow training is done in the summer and the autumn, when skiing still seems a long way off. Thus psychological strengths such as will, determination, stability, and patience are vital.

MAXIMUM CAPACITY VERSUS REQUIREMENTS

Maximum capacity can be expressed as a combination of physical and psychological abilities available in any one person.

Requirements means the particular combination of physical and psychological demands to be met in any one event.

Comparing a person's maximum capacity against the requirements of an event indicates individual strengths and weaknesses, and thus sets the goals for individual training for that event.

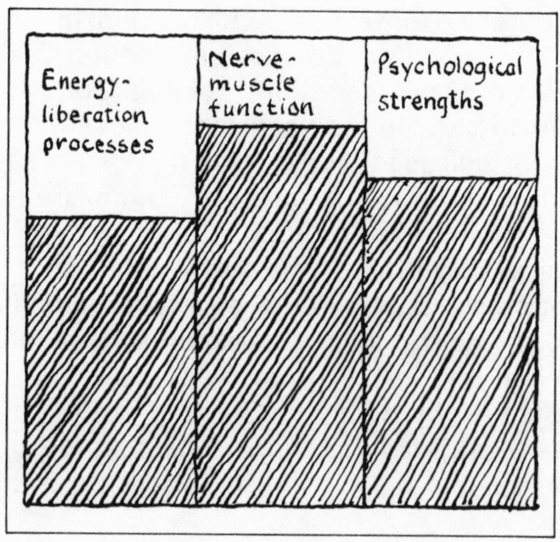

For illustration, assume that the requirements of cross-country can be drawn as a square, with the top edge being the desired ability level. A typical racer's maximum capacity is then plotted as shaded bars. The blank areas above the bars indicate where he is weak and thus in need of training. Of course this type of chart is only theoretical, as it is difficult if not impossible to measure all the abilities required and even more difficult to say just how much of each one is needed to ski well. Nonetheless, the purpose here is to show that training is not a single effort aimed at a single ability, but rather a combination of activities aimed at a common goal and organized in an individual manner. The requirements square shown is divided into abilities different from those used thus far in this book:

Energy-liberation processes: vital to endurance.

Nerve-muscle function: involves technique and muscular fitness.

Psychological strengths: mental and emotional.

The energy-liberation processes and certain aspects of muscular fitness can, to some extent, be tested and measured. Tests for this purpose are discussed at the end of this chapter.

TRAINING ABCs

Who and Why

To be a good touring skier or cross-country racer, you simply must ski a lot. A lot of skiing involves a lot of exercise, which requires a level of fitness which, in turn, is maintained by regular exercise. Even if you don't want to excel but merely want to enjoy recreational touring, you should have a level of fitness that allows you to tour without undue fatigue.

In any case, regularity in exercise is important to making touring skiing enjoyable and vital to making successful cross-country racing possible. In modern cross-country, systematic and constructive off-snow training, summer and fall, and on-snow training prior to the racing season are vital to successful winter racing. In fact, training is what has made cross-country racing a young person's sport.

Time was when cross-country racing was for hardened oldsters, veterans of the endurance events. Both men's and women's events were dominated by athletes in their thirties. But the ages of successful competitors have been steadily decreasing, chiefly because of year-round, more scientific training in all competing countries. In the 1972 Sapporo Winter Olympics, the age decrease was dramatic. The average age of the top five in the 15-kilometer race was twenty-three. Competing in their first Olympics, Czech Helena Siklova, twenty-one, took a bronze medal in the 5-kilometer, and Norwegian Ivar Formo, twenty, won a bronze in the 15-kilometer. Just a few days after his twenty-fourth birthday, Swede Thomas Magnusson won the 1974 FIS World Ski Championship 30-kilometer race ahead of many seasoned veterans, including Olympic medalists at the distance.

Despite the overwhelming evidence of the effect of systematic training in cross-country racing, training is not only for racers. It is for everyone who wants to enjoy skiing, be it leisurely touring or competitive racing. Efficient and enjoyable training is chiefly aimed at building up or maintaining endurance fitness, is regular, and is individual:

Endurance fitness dominates in touring and cross-country.

Regularity in exercise is vital. Irregular, sporadic exercise cannot build and will not maintain endurance fitness.

Individual training is a must. Your training, or your personal physical fitness program, must suit your level of fitness and your needs.

The training methods and programs presented in the rest of this chapter are those currently in use by serious touring skiers and cross-country racers in Norway. The principles are valid for all touring training.

However, if you've never exercised regularly before or are "completely out of shape," then it might be best to start with a jogging* or aerobics† type of program. In any case, it's a good idea to have a medical check-up and your doctor's go-ahead before you start an exercise program.

How, When, and Where . . .

The intensity of activity in any one period of a training program should be less than your maximum ability if it is to build up fitness. Tempo, or the speed at which you move, is usually no more than 50 to 60 percent of your maximum, although short exercise periods or tours can be run at greater tempo. The intensity and length of exercise periods increase as training progresses from summer through fall toward winter. Correct training is that which enables you to tolerate this increased intensity and length without feeling more tired or fatigued than earlier in the year.

The best place to train for cross-country is in the same surroundings as those of winter races. Thus you experience on foot some of the same variation as you would on skis.

Training should be enjoyable, something to look forward to, not something to bear as a chore. Summer recreation such as swimming, hiking, cycling, rowing, canoeing, squash, and soccer have training value and are psychologically stimulating.

---

*W. J. Bowerman and W. E. Harris, *Jogging* (New York: Grosset & Dunlap, 1967), $1.00.

†K. H. Cooper, *Aerobics* and *The New Aerobics* (New York: Bantam Books, 1968, 1970), $1.00 and $1.25.

What . . .

A cross-country skier must be able to endure. Endurance training takes time, both to maintain and to improve endurance fitness. Thus, long training periods are characteristic of cross-country training.

Cross-country also demands special muscle strengths. Fortunately these strengths can be built up and maintained mostly during endurance training with the correct muscle-movement patterns, that is, movements which are exactly like or similar to those used on skis. Most off-snow endurance training is done on foot, so it must be supplemented with strength training for arms and upper-body muscles, as cross-country uses arms as well as legs. In the last few years, cross-country skiers have done most of their arm-strength training on roller skis, which combine endurance and strength training.

Exercises aimed at limbering up or stretching do not directly produce better on-ski race results. But stretching after exercising is valuable, because muscles must be at their proper working lengths to prevent tendon damage. A cross-country racer usually develops all the agility and resilience necessary simply by running and skiing in varying terrain.

A racer must have good technique to race well. Technique practice can be separate from physical training, but physical ability and good technique depend on one another. Usually racers practice technique on skis as a part of endurance training.

EXERCISE PHYSIOLOGY

Modern training programs rely heavily on work physiology, and many physiological expressions have come into common use in recreation and athletics. Aerobic and anaerobic are the two most important terms used in describing overall fitness.

Aerobic processes require air for energy liberation and transfer. Air enters the body into the lungs where oxygen is transferred to the blood. The heart pumps blood to various parts of the body, including the skeletal muscles. Oxygen absorbed from the blood is "burned" by the muscles as they work. In aerobic processes,

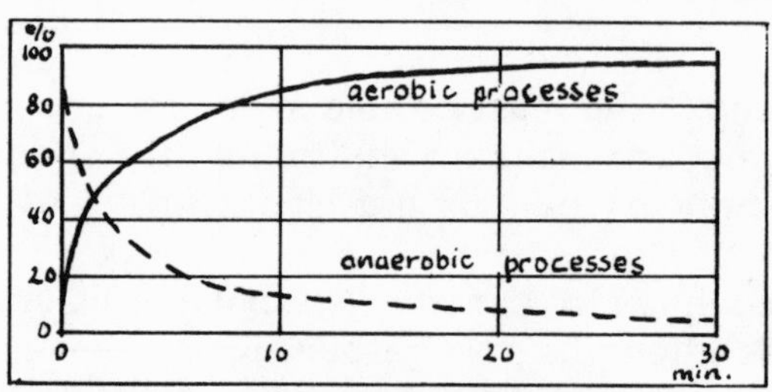

Distribution of aerobic and anaerobic processes depend on the duration of exercise.

oxygen is then necessary for transferring the chemically bound energy to mechanical energy in the muscles.

The more oxygen-containing blood is pumped to the muscles, the more energy can be transferred into mechanical movement. Thus the heart's "fitness level" is important in the body's ability to process oxygen and liberate energy. The body's ability to liberate energy over long periods of time is equivalent to its ability to perform work over long periods of time.

Energy liberation and transfer processes are thus important in endurance. The body's ability to take up oxygen, "aerobic endurance," is an important part of endurance. Aerobic endurance is, in turn, dependent on cardiovascular capability.

Aerobic training is designed to maintain or increase aerobic endurance, a vital ability in cross-country racing.

Anaerobic means literally "without air"; the energy transfer and liberation processes involved function without oxygen. The chief sources of energy for muscular movement are carbohydrates and fat from food consumed. The anaerobic process, instead of "burning" carbohydrates, chiefly involves a breakdown of the glucose molecule to lactate. The process is inefficient when compared to the aerobic process: on a weight basis, glucose liberates roughly twenty times as much energy aerobically as anaerobically. In addition, the lactic acid produced by the anaerobic process must be removed. That which does not enter the circulating blood (for transfer primarily to the liver) can remain in the muscles. Thus the anaerobic process can leave its own type of residue.

Anaerobic processes dominate in short-duration, high-load

efforts. Longer-duration work cannot be so intense, and thus must be aerobic.

Whenever muscles go from rest to motion, or from motion with light load to motion with heavy load, their demand for energy transfer increases. The aerobic processes are relatively slow in starting, so sudden increased demands for energy transfer are met by anaerobic processes for the first minute or so. Cross-country racers skiing from a flat onto an uphill create just such a demand for anaerobic power.

Every individual has a maximum limit for energy transfer via aerobic processes which is called maximum oxygen uptake. But energy transfer can be increased above that available aerobically by anaerobic muscle work. Anaerobic endurance is the ability to perform work when oxygen supply is inadequate or the oxygen transfer has reached its maximum.

Anaerobic training is aimed at maintaining or increasing anaerobic endurance. It's difficult to state any one ideal relation between anaerobic and aerobic endurance for a cross-country racer. The amount of anaerobic and aerobic work in a race depend on the course profile. Assuming similar work loads, the aerobic and anaerobic functions can be summarized as follows:

Anaerobic processes are most important for short-duration, high-intensity work, up to 2 minutes.

Aerobic processes are more important for longer-duration work.

Work periods which vary from 2 to 10 minutes usually involve both anaerobic and aerobic processes.

Work periods exceeding 10 minutes involve mostly aerobic processes.

PULSE—THE INDICATOR

Almost all training programs aimed at overall fitness use pulse rate as a measure of exercise intensity and thus as a measure of the benefit of the training involved.

But pulse rate is individual; the same pulse rate does not mean the same level of physical fitness or exercise intensity for different persons. This is chiefly because the maximum heart rate is individual. For instance, if two persons exercise, each at a pulse rate of 170 beats per minute, they can be training quite differently. If one has a maximum heart rate of 170 beats per minute and the other a maximum rate of 210 beats per minute, then the first man is working at or near his maximum while the second is working at a lower intensity.

Maximum Heart Rate

Maximum heart rate is an expression often used in discussing exercise. The heart rate is the number of ventricular beats per minute. A person's maximum heart rate is the maximum number of times his heart's chambers empty and fill per minute under a demanding work load such as running. The heart rate is most easily measured by checking the pulse rate, which is the number of pressure waves per minute along the arteries. In normal, healthy persons, the pulse rate equals the heart rate.

Training does not increase the maximum heart rate, nor is there any evidence that a high or low maximum heart rate is or is not desirable or advantageous in endurance events. The maximum heart rate varies from person to person, and, for any one person, decreases with age. Persons in their twenties, for example, will have maximum heart rates from 170 to 220.

Thus you can get an indication of exercise intensity by checking pulse rate if you know your own maximum heart rate. You can determine your maximum heart rate as follows:

1. Warm up thoroughly.

2. Foot-run on a solid, hard surface that is either flat or slightly uphill. Run at top but even speed for 4 to 5 minutes, preferably at a full sprint the last minute.

3. Stop and count your pulse immediately. Count beats for 6 seconds and multiply by 10, or count for 10 seconds and multiply by 6.

The resultant number of beats per minute is your approximate maximum heart rate. It is important to count immediately after you stop running and to count for only 6 to 10 seconds, as the heart

Right: Pulse watches give the most accurate pulse counts.

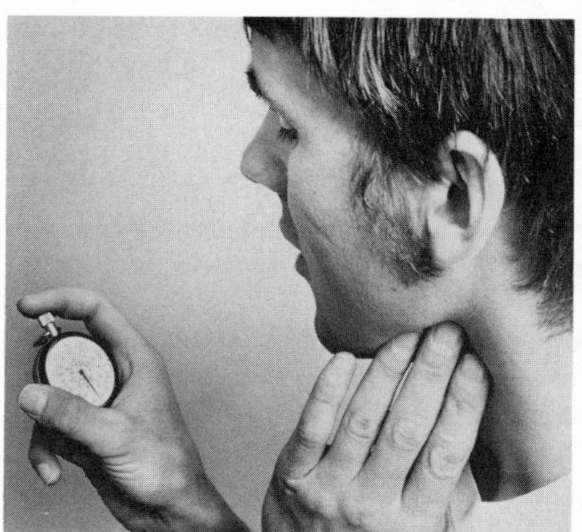

slows down immediately after exercise ceases. Repeat the above process as a check.

Taking Your Pulse

Take your pulse by pressing fingers lightly on the carotid artery (main artery in the neck) next to the trachea (air tube). The pulse can also be felt by placing the hand on the chest over the heart; this is a good method for slender persons.

Count for 6 to 10 seconds, preferably using a watch or clock with a sweep second hand or a stopwatch. Recently, some watchmakers have marketed pulse watches which give a far more accurate count than possible by the counting and multiplying method. These watches are simply started on a pulse beat and stopped after a specified number of beats, usually 10 or 15. The pulse rate is then read directly on the watch face.

WARMING UP AND MOVING

Training for ski touring and cross-country ski racing is organized to improve endurance, muscular fitness, and technique. However these are not necessarily separate programs because fitness and technique training are designed to increase endurance as well. In all training *warming up* is essential before every exercise period, and all *movements* are aimed at the goal of bettering or maintaining the ability to perform skiing movements.

Warming Up

Warming up before training both minimizes the chance of injury and enables you to get the greatest benefit from a training period.

Warming up need not be any particular set of exercises. You can warm up at the start of a training session simply by beginning slowly and easily; on foot just jog, and on skis just ski easily and slowly. When you feel that you are loosened up, then you can start training.

Easy, relaxed stretching exercises are also good for warming up, and are ideal before strength training. After warm-up, it's best to start strength training with a moderate load before going on to the full program load.

A period of 15 to 30 minutes is needed for warming up the circulatory system and the body muscles before they can work at their maximum.

A long training tour can start slowly with a warm-up jog. Warming up is especially important before a race.

Exercises—Some Old, Some New

Endurance training can be done on skis or on foot. The movements on skis are like touring, as described in Chapter 2. The movements on foot are walking, jogging and running, and imitation training as described below.

Muscular fitness and mobility training use some of the movements of endurance training plus calisthenics specifically designed for skiing muscles.

WALKING In exercising, you should walk

—during the initial minutes of warming up

—for a whole training tour if your fitness is low or the tour is extremely long

—off trails or paths in wilderness areas

—in extremely steep terrain

—during rests in interval and tempo training (defined on pages 125 and 126)

Use your normal walk, preferably loose and relaxed with a springy step. Try to walk with your feet pointing straight forward: avoid duck-footed or pigeon-toed walking.

JOGGING AND RUNNING These are used primarily in endurance training, though sometimes in muscular-fitness training. Jog or run naturally. On longer tours, try to land on your heel with toes pointed up, and then roll over to your toe for the next kick. Too much running on your toes on longer tours may overtax and thus injure calf muscles and tendons.

"Ski Striding"—Imitation Training

Ski striding is a variation of walking or running done uphill to imitate skiing. The same muscles, ligaments, tendons, and joints work in the same movement patterns used in the diagonal stride on skis. Ski striding is divided into "normal ski striding," which resembles walking, and "bounding ski striding," which resembles running. Both varieties can be done without or with poles. Ski strides are used chiefly in endurance training but also are valuable in muscular-fitness training.

Ski striding imitates the skiing diagonal stride as it is correctly done on the flat or up gentle uphills. Ski striding resembles ordinary walking, except that the kick should be stronger, the step longer, and the leading knee bent more. The upper body should lean a bit forward from the hips, the feet should point forward,

Normal ski stride without poles

and the leading foot should land on its heel. The hip, knee, and ankle stretch out quickly in the kick, just as they do on skis. All movements should be rhythmic, and the arms should swing pendulumlike forward and back.

Normal ski striding meets the athletic definition of walking in that one foot should always be in contact with the ground. Think of skiing while ski striding.

Ski striding with poles is excellent as endurance and muscular fitness training for the arm and upper-body muscles when done several times up a steep hill.

The underlying ground surface should be even, such as a good dirt road or well-worn, broad trail. The body position and leg work are the same as for normal ski striding without poles. Arms and poles work as in the diagonal stride on skis. Pole length should be about 2 inches less than normal pole length for skiing.

Bounding ski striding is good muscular-resilience training when done several times up a steep hill. The movements are similar to those of the normal ski stride, but are quicker and more powerful, as in uphill diagonal striding on skis. The bounding ski stride meets the athletic definition of running, because the runner is airborne with both feet off the ground just before landing on his forward foot. The landing should be on the heel, with a roll-over to the toe for the next kick. The body should lean slightly forward, and arms should work as in the normal ski stride.

Bounding ski striding with poles is also useful as resilience training when done several times uphill. The body position and arm movements are similar to those of the normal ski stride with poles, except the runner is airborne just before landing on the heel of his forward foot. This stride is the most like skiing, so think of skiing as you stride.

Bounding ski stride with poles

Roller Skis

Roller skis are a bit like giant roller skates, and are attached to the foot with standard cross-country toe bindings and boots. The wheels are fitted with ratchets that prevent the skis from rolling backward. The skis should be used on paved surfaces with poles about the same length as those used on snow. Almost all cross-country movements can be done on roller skis, but they are most useful for double poling and diagonal striding, movements otherwise absent in off-ski training. Training on roller skis is chiefly for muscle fitness but it also has some value in endurance training.

Other Useful Nonskiing Activities

Cycling, rowing, and canoeing are excellent as variation in endurance training. Cycling and rowing are also good endurance-strength training for leg and back muscles. Canoeing has some value as arm-strength training for cross-country ski racing.

ENDURANCE TRAINING

Touring skiers and cross-country ski racers endurance-train by walking, running, jogging, or ski striding on foot, and by skiing.

Endurance training involves minimum exercise intensities over time periods long enough to achieve the desired training goal, of which there are three, involving three types of training:

Distance training is a continuous pace, foot running, jogging, or skiing of at least half and usually not more than twice the duration of a ski race. Its purpose is to build up aerobic capacity.

Interval training is running, ski striding, or skiing composed of a series of intense but relatively short exercise periods separated from one another by rest intervals of shorter duration. Its purpose is to build up anaerobic capacity, and to increase the ability to tolerate the transition from aerobic to anaerobic exercise.

Tempo training is running or skiing at racing speeds or greater for periods equaling 10 to 20 percent of a race's duration. Its purpose is to enable the body to tolerate high lactic-acid concentrations over longer periods of time as well as accustoming the skier to racing speeds.

In other words, endurance training involves both long tours run at low tempo and shorter tours run at higher tempo. Long tours are run at one-half to two-thirds maximum speed, while shorter tours are run at three-fourths to full maximum speed.

Because men, women, and boys and girls race different distances, the maximum length of their endurance training periods differ:

Left: Two types of roller ski. Light type in foreground has three small, solid-rubber tires and is best for use on asphalt or similar hard surfaces. Slightly heavier type in background has two larger balloon tires, and can be used on rougher surfaces such as dirt roads.

Below: Roller skiing on asphalt. Note that poles have no baskets and are equipped with hardened steel tips.

Long Exercise Periods

2 to 3 hours for men

2 hours for women

1 hour for boys and girls

Best done as continuous-movement *distance training* at one-half maximum speed.

Short Exercise Periods

½ to 1½ hours for adults

¼ to ½ hour for boys and girls

Done as continuous-movement *distance training* at three-fourths maximum speed, or

Interval training at three-fourths maximum speed in each sprint, or

Tempo training at maximum speed in each sprint.

Training for cross-country racing is best done in terrain similar to that used for race courses. The different types of terrain encountered in courses may be classified into four groups:

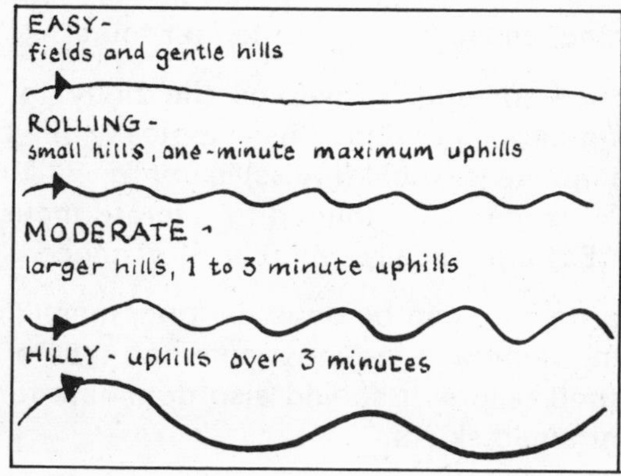

Distance Training

MOVEMENT Skiing, walking, running, jogging, ski striding, roller skiing, and, as variation, rowing and cycling.

INTENSITY Generally intensity should be continuous and even, although uphills may be a bit tougher than flats and downhills, both on foot and on skis. Uphills should *not* be run so hard that muscles stiffen. Specifically, intensity as measured by pulse rate depends on the length of exercise period involved as shown in the chart below:

		Duration of Period in Hours and Approximate Pulse Rate (higher on uphills, lower on downhills)		
Exercise Duration	Speed	Boys and Girls	Women, 18 and Older; Men, 18 and 19	Men, 20 and Older
Long	½ max.	1 hour at 140 pulse	2 hours at 135 pulse	2–3 hours at 135 pulse
Short	¾ max.	½ hour at 175 pulse	½–1 hour at 165 pulse	1–1½ hours at 165 pulse

Beginning cross-country racers and skiers at lower physical fitness levels should *walk* the longer training periods.

CHOICE OF TERRAIN Easy or rolling terrain is recommended for distance training, especially for the longer tours.

EFFECT Distance training accustoms the body to continuous effort over long periods of time. Physiologically, the body's maximum oxygen uptake (aerobic fitness) is improved. Muscles, ligaments, and joints are strengthened to tolerate thousands of repeated loads. Psychologically, the fear of distance is reduced.

USE Distance training can be done on long, medium, and short tours. Distance training is the most common type of endurance training for good racers. It should also dominate for beginning racers and untrained skiers.

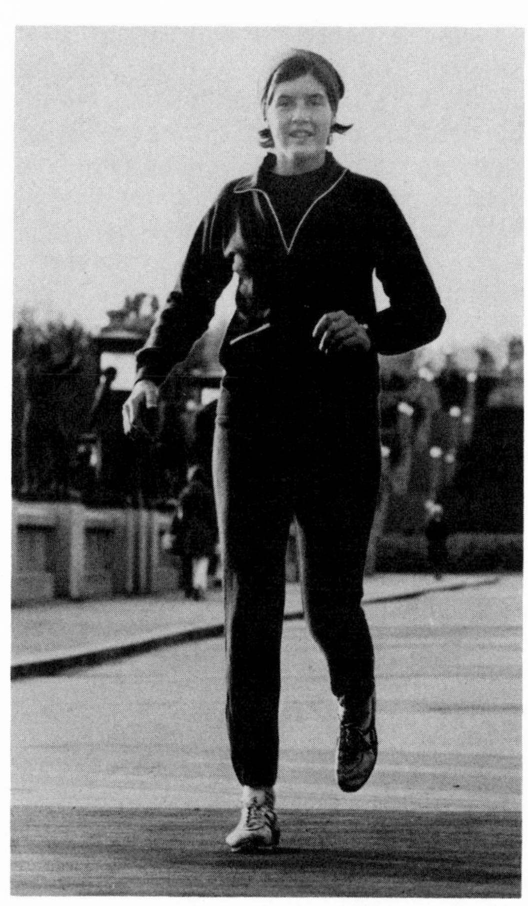

Interval Training

MOVEMENT Skiing, walking, bounding ski stride, jogging, running, roller skiing, and, as variation, cycling in moderate terrain.

INTENSITY Interval training is a series of intense but relatively short exercise periods, or sprints, separated from one another by rest intervals of shorter duration. There are two general types of interval training: *timed interval* in which the sprints and rests follow a definite timed sequence on a track or up and down a single hill, and *natural interval* as done in undulating terrain where uphills and downhills provide the sprints and rests. Timed interval is further broken up into short interval and long interval, according to the duration of the sprints and rests. Short interval is known as "windsprinting" in track and field athletics, while long interval and natural interval are usually used only by cross-country skiers and cross-country foot runners.

Short Intervals

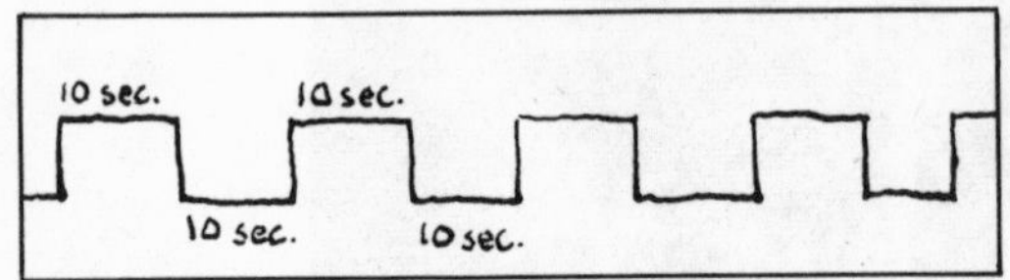

Sprint length: 10 to 60 seconds

Rest length: 5 to 15 seconds

Sprints and rests should correspond:

If sprint length is	Then rest length should be	
10 sec.	10 sec. or less	
15 sec.	15 sec. or less	
20 sec.	15 sec. or less	
30 sec.	15 sec.	Difficult because muscles may stiffen quickly. This form of interval may be "too tough."
60 sec.	15 sec.	

Untrained: One or two series, 5 minutes each

Well trained: Three series, 10 minutes each

Four-minute rests between series

INTENSITY The first sprints should seem easy. The last sprints in each series should be just about but not quite make you stiff. Pulse rate should be at or near maximum for 3 to 10 minutes in each series.

EFFORT The total effort should be the same in all sprints of all series of any one training period. If you can't maintain speed, take a longer rest or stop training for the day.

Long Intervals

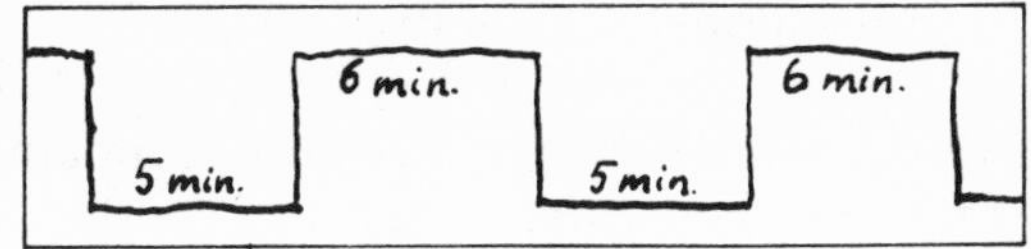

Sprint length: 2½ to 8 minutes

Rest length: Approximately same as but preferably shorter than sprint length. In moderate terrain where sprints are 3½ minutes or longer, rests can be longer than sprints.

INTENSITY You should feel a bit stiff at the end of each sprint and be a little out of breath. Pulse rate should be at maximum or 5 to 15 beats per minute under maximum at the end of each sprint.

EFFORT Effort should be the same in all sprints. If you can't maintain speed, stop training for the day.

Total training time
Adults: 30 to 60 minutes
Boys and girls: 20 to 35 minutes

Untrained: Three sprints, 4 minutes each

Well trained: Up to ten sprints, 4 minutes each

Natural Intervals Sprint and rest lengths depend on terrain and ground conditions.

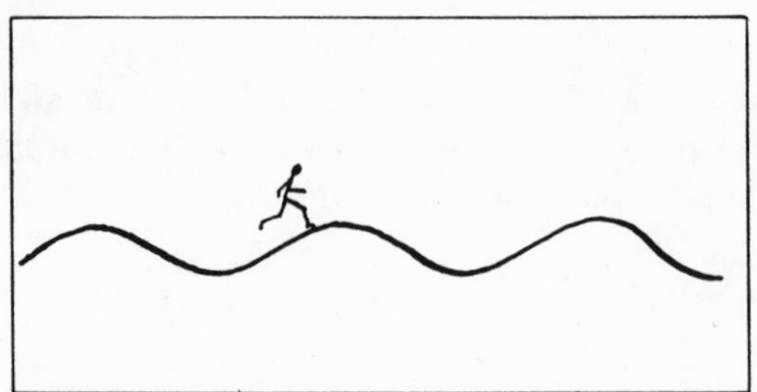

Intensity should be such that you are a little stiff at the end of the longest uphills. Pulse rate should be close to maximum at the end of the three or four longest uphills in each tour.

Total training time should be 30 to 90 minutes for adults, and 15 to 40 minutes for boys and girls. Longer tours, up to 90 minutes, are acceptable if the rests are extra long as, for instance, on long flat stretches.

CHOICE OF TERRAIN The best terrain is moderate with hills of varying length. Ideally, the profile should be the same as that for a cross-country ski race. Downhills should be on a firm base; if you slip and slide on downhills and have to go slowly, the pauses will be too long. If your training program has no long interval training, then your natural interval tours should include a few hills of 3 to 4 minutes' length or more.

Effect of Interval Training Short intervals are cardiovascular training and are aimed at increasing maximum oxygen uptake.

Long intervals also increase maximum oxygen uptake. In addition, long intervals teach ability to ration strength correctly to ski long hills in races.

Natural intervals: Uphills of 3½ minutes or more function as long intervals. Terrain variations are psychologically stimulating, as you meet the same sort of variation in effort as required in a race. In moderate terrain, natural intervals are more like short intervals.

Use of Interval Training Short intervals provide variation in training, especially in short-duration, high-intensity training in the fall, but also in on-ski training in moderate terrain.

Long intervals are ideal for building up maximum oxygen uptake. Experienced racers often ski stride up and jog down the same hill several times for long interval training.

Natural intervals are ideal for all racers, and are the most used by experienced racers.

Hard, interval-only training should not be done at the expense of distance training. Never train intervals more than three times a week.

Ski Striding as Pure Interval Training This form of interval training is done up and down a single hill. Ski stride or bounding ski stride with poles up the hill, then jog down. "Up" sprints and "down" rests should be of about the same length. The lengths are, of course, dependent on the hill involved, but should usually be between 45 seconds and 5 to 6 minutes. The longest sprints are a form of long interval training, and should be done with ski stride only. The shorter sprints, 45 seconds to 2 minutes, are best done in a bounding ski stride with poles.

The bounding ski stride with poles also is good endurance training for the muscle groups most often used in cross-country ski racing, making it a good variation in basic endurance training.

Intensity should be at a level that allows you to recover well while jogging downhill to your starting point. If you reach a point when you don't seem to have the energy to start a new uphill sprint, then stop for the day.

Duration depends on the hill involved and on your training level. Approximate total training times are:

Men, senior: 20 to 60 minutes total

Women, senior, and men, junior: 15 to 30 minutes total

Boys and girls and all untrained skiers: 15 to 20 minutes

Tempo Training

Tempo training is training aimed at enabling you to maintain the speed required in a race. Note: Tempo training is recommended only for competing athletes, not for recreational skiers.

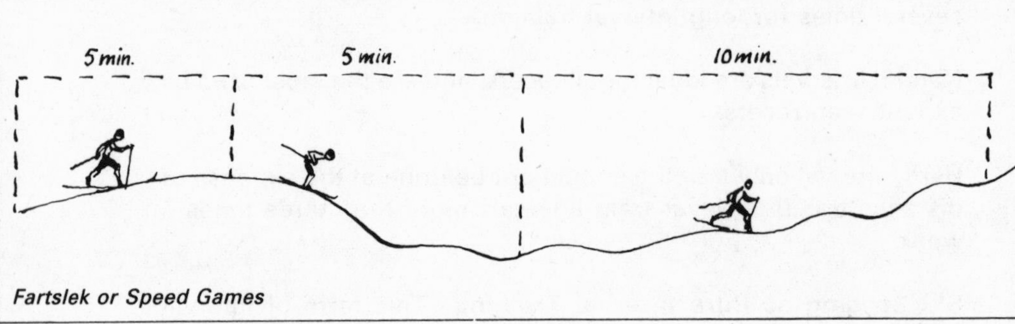

Fartslek or Speed Games

MOVEMENT Skiing, bounding ski stride, running.

GENERAL Tempo training is a systematic series of high-intensity, short-duration exercise and longer rests. It is divided up into short and long tempo according to the duration of the exercise periods.

Short Tempo

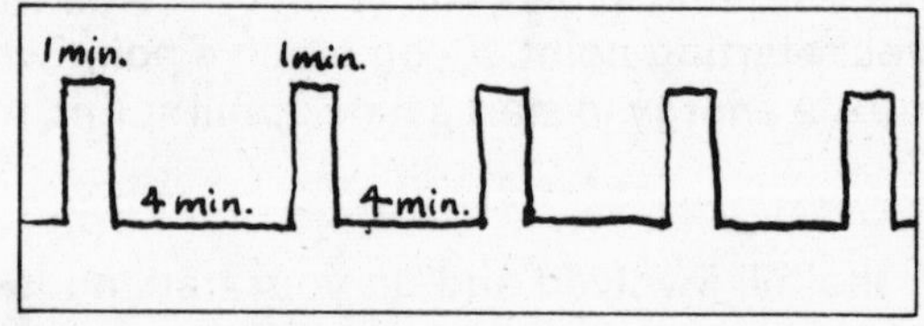

Sprint length: 50 to 80 seconds

Rest length: 4 minutes

Total number of sprints: 2 to 4

Long Tempo

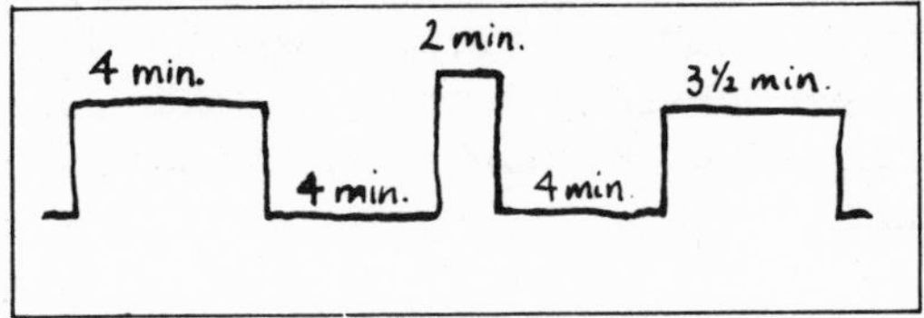

Sprint length: 1½ to 10 minutes

Rest length: 4 to 6 minutes

Total number of sprints: 1 to 4

Combined Short-Long Tempo

Combination of short and long, 2 to 4 sprints total

Natural Tempo: "Fartslek"

Sprints in varying terrain and/or ski tracks

Sprint length: 5 to 15 minutes

Rest length (jogging or easy skiing): 5 to 15 minutes

Total number of sprints: 1 to 3

MUSCULAR FITNESS AND SPEED TRAINING

Warm up thoroughly before muscular-fitness or speed training.

Muscular-fitness training involves specific exercises for strength and resilience.

Principles of Muscle-strength Training

The basic principle of muscle-strength training is that increased load and thus increased muscle effort are necessary to increase muscle strength. For the purposes of cross-country skiing, muscle strength can be thought of as maximum strength and repetitive, or endurance strength.

Increased resistance is requisite to increasing muscle strength. But excess resistance can injure.

Maximum strength is measured in terms of the greatest resistance a muscle can overcome in one effort. Weight lifters, for instance, need great maximum strength. The basic principle in building maximum strength is heavy loads—lifting, pushing, or pulling—and few repetitions of movement, seldom more than 3 to 6 in each series.

Repetitive strength is measured in terms of the muscular ability to overcome a moderate resistance many times. Cross-country skiers need great repetitive strength. The basic principle of training repetitive strength is moderate loads and many repetitions of movement.

Principles of Resilience Training

Resilience and strength are related to one another, and thus are often discussed as one quality. For the purposes of cross-country skiing, muscle strength is measured by the resistance a muscle can overcome. Resilience, on the other hand, determines how high one can jump, how far one can jump, how rapid one can kick on skis, and so on.

Resilience depends on strength; muscles give the power to perform movement. A cross-country skier trains resilience for diagonal striding in the bounding ski stride.

Resilience training involves maximum effort in each movement, each kick, and short exercise periods separated by long rest periods. These rest periods can be used to stretch and limber up. As soon as you feel a bit fatigued and can't maintain speed, take an extra long rest, 3 to 5 minutes. This happens normally after 7 exercise periods.

Principles of Speed Training

Speed training aims at attaining high speed. Boxers, for instance, speed-train to punch rapidly, and sprinters speed-train to run fast. Sprinters must not only kick rapidly and hard on each step, but they must also take quick strides, or have a high tempo. Therefore speed depends on resilience and strength.

But speed training should not be confused with tempo training. Speed training helps you raise your own level of speed, and tempo training helps you keep it up.

There is no one specific speed training for cross-country skiers. Cross-country movements contribute to both resilience and speed, and learning good technique is in itself a form of speed training. Taking short sprints at high speed on skis using good technique is thus the best specific speed training.

Leg Training—The Stretch Movement

Walking and running in rugged terrain are generally regarded as endurance training, but they also have value as repetitive strength training for leg muscles.

The bounding ski stride is useful as strength and resilience training for cross-country skiers. When used as resilience training, the activity program should be:

Several relatively short (10 to 15 seconds) sprints up a steep hill

Easy walk down between sprints

Long rest (3 to 5 minutes) as soon as you tire or movements slow down

Usual pattern: 3 series of 5 to 7 sprints each

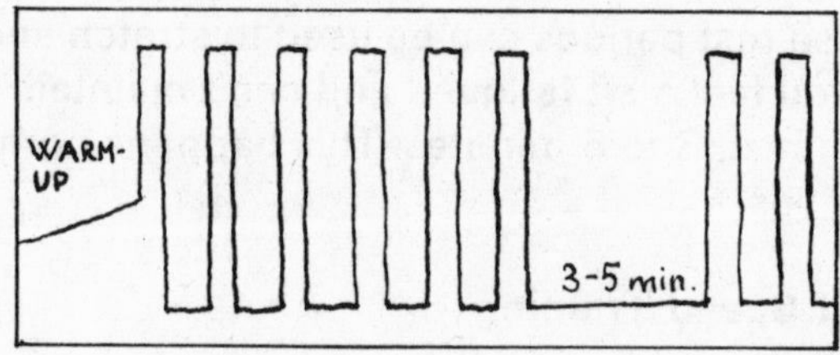

Uphill sprinting has about the same effect as the bounding ski stride, and should be done following the same program as outlined immediately above. Because it lacks some of skiing's movements, however, uphill sprinting is not regarded as being equal to bounding ski striding in training value—but it is useful as a movement variation in strength-and-resilience leg-muscle training.

Weight training, such as barbell squats, can be used to advantage (see Exercise 8 on page 147). Untrained persons should use lighter weights. If you are well trained or are experienced with weights, heavier weights and fewer repetitions can be useful.

Rowing and cycling are primarily enjoyable variations in distance training, but both are useful as strength-and-resilience training for leg and back muscles.

Arm and Upper-body Training—The Poling Movements

If you could ski all year round, your arms and upper body would most likely not need any other form of training. Therefore, unless your arms and upper body are especially weak, skiing alone is adequate for winter training. If you are weak, you can ski emphasizing arm movements; for example, try double poling on all flats on one-third of your training tours.

Roller skis provide an efficient method of training arms and upper-body muscles in skiing movements. Although some roller skis available today (1974–75 season) allow you to do all skiing strides, they are heavier than racing skis. Therefore you should train chiefly double poling and double pole striding, concentrating on poling movements. Ski on the flat and on a few gradual uphills.

Arm-training devices are various mechanisms designed to load arm muscles in the diagonal-stride or double-pole rhythms. There are three main types:

Diagonal-stride arm training

Weight on rails (see Weight Exercise 6 on page 145). Weights on slanted rails with ropes running over pulleys at 7 to 8 feet above ground provide a resistance pattern very nearly like that of poling on skis. However, these devices are usually found only in well-equipped gyms or training centers, and must be maintained carefully if they are to work properly.

Elastic or rubber cords can be pulled in both the double-poling and diagonal-stride movements. They should be regarded as pure strength training, as they provide resistance different from that of poling. In poling, resistance is greatest in the initial pull phase just after the pole has been planted and then decreases to almost nothing at the end of the push phase. Elastic and rubber cords give an increasing resistance as the arm swings backward, which is just the opposite of the poling resistance pattern.

Cord-resistance devices consist of nylon cords passing around one or more of the four spokes of a metal hub mounted about 7 feet above ground. Cord friction is greater at standstill than when moving, so these devices duplicate the ski poling resistance pattern. But they can be used only for diagonal arm movements.

Suggested Arm-training Period Using Arm-training Devices
Regulate resistance so that your arm movements are on the verge of being lethargic toward the end of each series. If possible (with the first two devices), vary between diagonal movements one day, and double-poling movements the next.

Start with four 30-second series using medium resistance; rests of 1 minute between series

3-minute rest

Three 15-second series at maximum resistance with 1-minute rest between series

3-minute rest

One 1½-minute series at low resistance

Resistance can be increased as strength increases. Well-trained skiers can run through a whole program in diagonal movement, rest 10 minutes, and then run through the program again in double poling.

Other Exercises for Arm and Upper-body Training Ski striding is useful for arm and upper-body training. Normal ski striding with poles has more value as special repetitive-strength training for poling than it does as general endurance training. When concentrating on arm training, choose relatively steep hills and stride using powerful arm movements. For variation, try hills of different length. The bounding ski stride with poles has more value as general endurance training than it does as special arm training.

Often, bounding ski stride sprints are so intense that you feel weak all over when you finish. Therefore, if you use the bounding ski stride as arm training, keep the uphill stretches short and quick and emphasize arm movement. When you tire, take a 3- to 5-minute rest.

Canoeing and rowing train general endurance and have value as strength training for skiing pole movements. Competition rowing is valuable for leg and back muscles and strengthens bicep and tricep arm muscles and thus has some value for cross-country skiing. *But beware: Rowing puts potentially dangerous loads on the lower spine which can injure and incapacitate.*

Speed Training

Speed training is best done on skis when you are completely rested but well warmed up. Short maximum-speed sprints using good technique serve as speed training. On the flat, these sprints can last ½ to 1½ minutes, but on uphills they should be limited to 10 to 30 seconds. Between sprints, ski easily for 2 to 3 minutes, but *concentrate continually on maintaining good technique.* Stop training when you can no longer maintain top speed in the sprints.

Stationary Strength-training Exercises

Strength training is designed to build up the required strengths in the different movement patterns necessary in cross-country. The exercises described here fall into two groups: those using body weight as a resistance and those using apparatus or weights as resistance.

The number of times an exercise is performed, or the total number of repetitions, should be an individual thing suited to your training program. There are two general ways of deciding how many repetitions you should do:

1. Try each exercise to see how many repetitions you can do. When training, do three-fourths of the maximum for each exercise, and run through 3 to 4 series of exercises with 1 to 2 minutes' rest between series. Test yourself each month to find your new maximums, and adjust your training accordingly.

2. Athletes accustomed to strength training can perform as

many repetitions as they feel they can do of each exercise, keeping going until movement becomes lethargic. Run through 3 to 4 series of exercises, with several minutes' rest between series.

Exercises Using Body Resistance

Exercise 1: *Sit-ups* (hip flexers)

Feet held down under chair rung, tree root, etc. Knees may be bent if desired, which makes the exercise more effective for abdominal muscles.

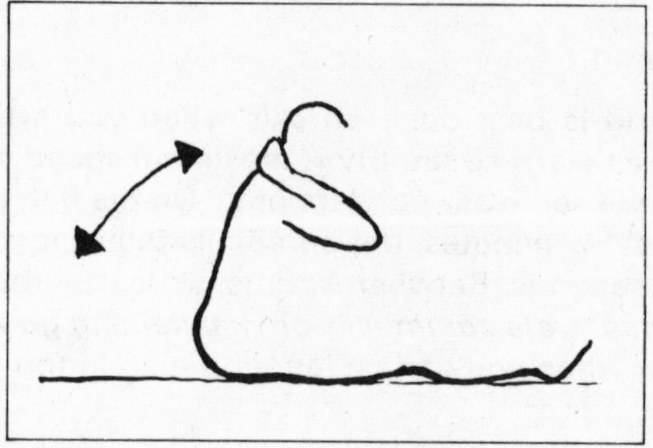

Exercise 2: *Arch sit-ups* (abdominal, frontal muscles)

Straight up or up with shoulder twist to one side.

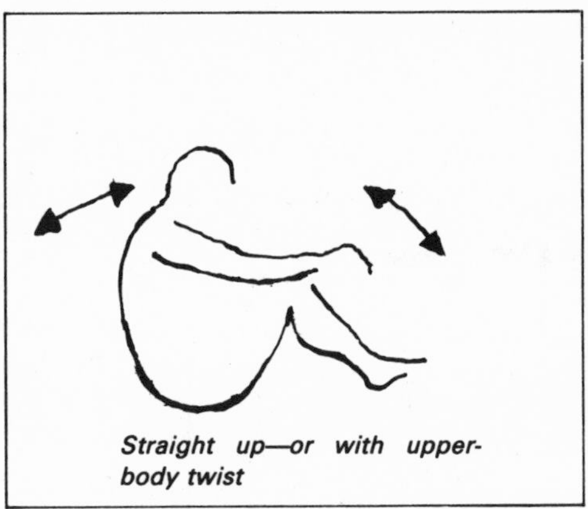

Straight up—or with upper-body twist

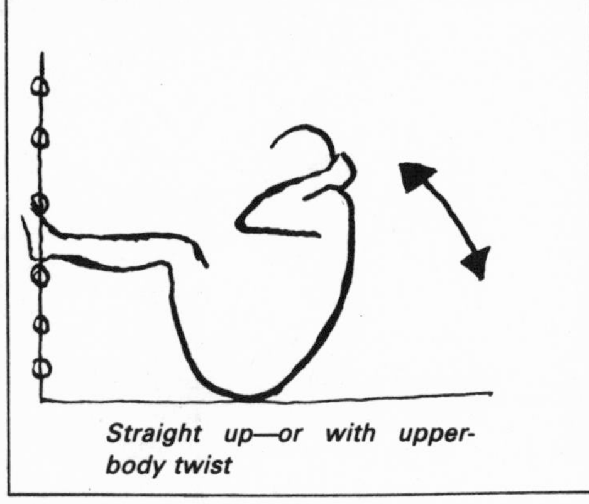

Straight up—or with upper-body twist

Exercise 3: *Back extension* (back muscles)

Lift head, elbows, and upper body. After gaining experience, use light weight (a sand sack will do) behind head.

With a helper

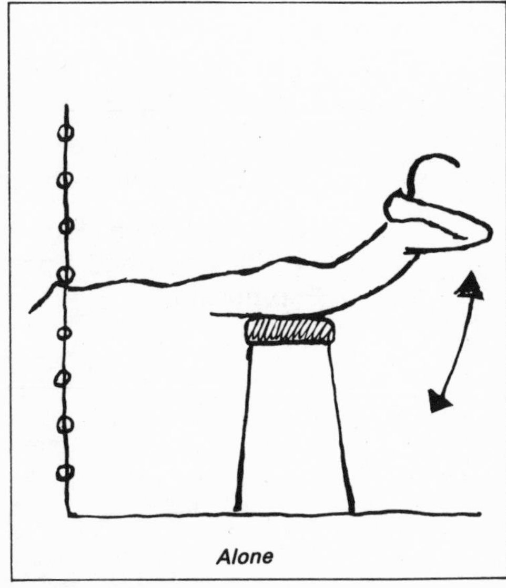

Alone

Exercise 4: *Pull-ups* (arms and upper-body muscles)

Straight down to chin over bar. Vary between overhand and underhand grip on bar.

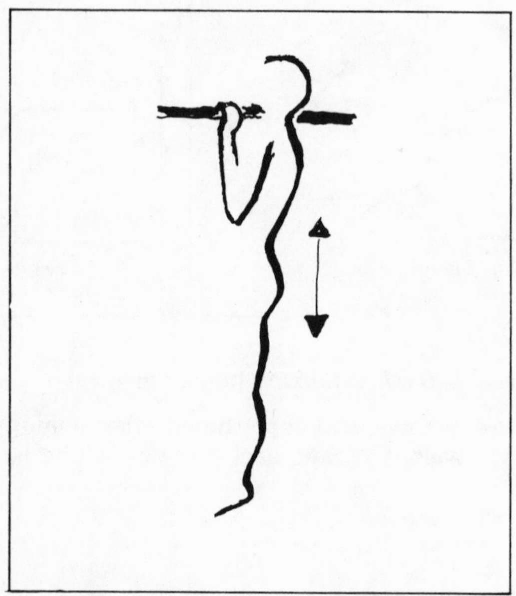

Exercise 5: *Push-ups* (elbow extenders—triceps)

Prone position, legs together, hands on floor at shoulder width with fingers pointing straight ahead. Straight body in up position.

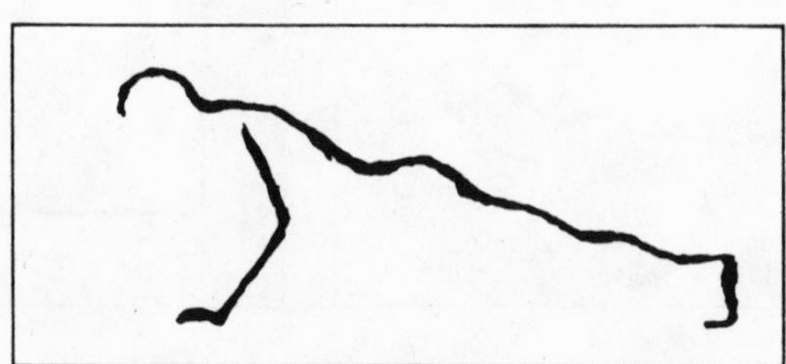

Exercises Using Apparatus

Exercise 6: *Arm training* (for poling movements)

Weights on rails with ropes over pulleys, elastic or rubber cords, or cord-friction apparatus, both diagonal and double-poling movements.

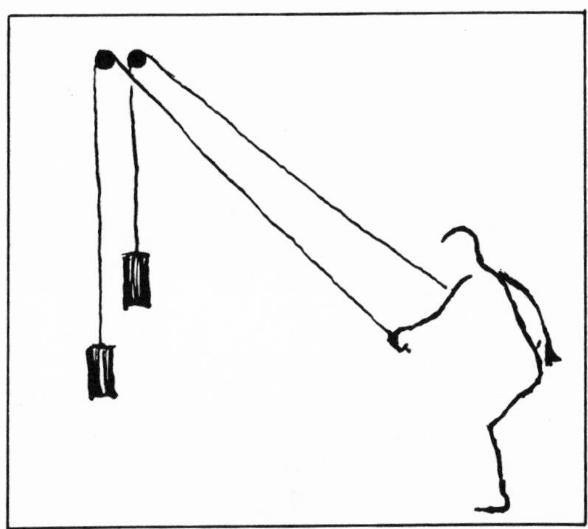

Exercise 7: *Barbell rowing* (upper arm, back-thrust movement)

Feet apart, knees slightly bent, back straight and parallel to floor. Grip barbell at shoulder width with overhand grip. Rapid lifts up to chest, slowly down to start position. Weight so you can do 25 to 50 repetitions.

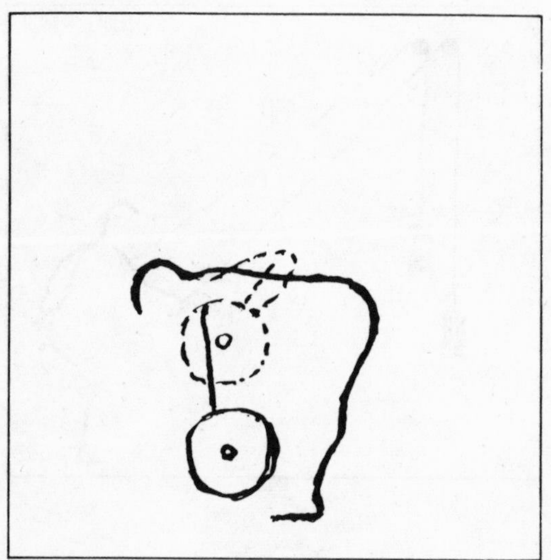

Exercise 8: *Barbell squat* (knee and hip extension)

Feet apart, barbell on back of shoulders, straight back. Slowly down and rapidly up. Avoid full squat, go no farther down than thighs parallel to floor. Weight so you can do 40 repetitions.

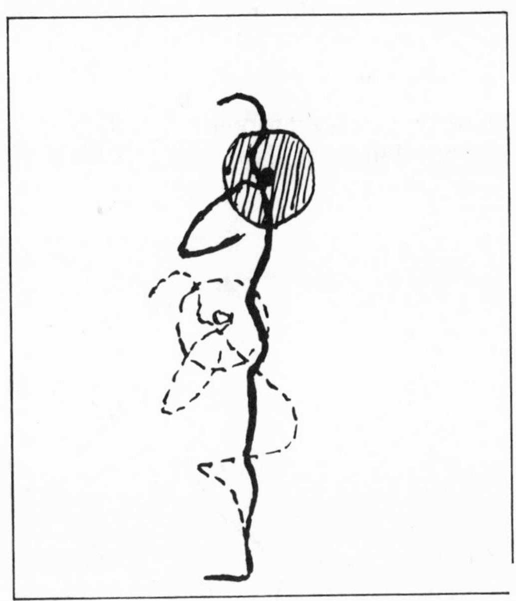

FLEXIBILITY TRAINING

Stretching or limbering-up exercises maintains or increases flexibility. They have their greatest effect when done strongly and deliberately, yet slowly. The best time to stretch is at the end of a strength- or endurance-training period. In all cases, *warm up thoroughly before extreme stretching.* The following stationary stretching exercises are useful in cross-country training.

Exercise 1: Inner thigh

Broad stance, feet straight forward, bend and straighten alternately right and left knee, feel stretch in inner thigh.

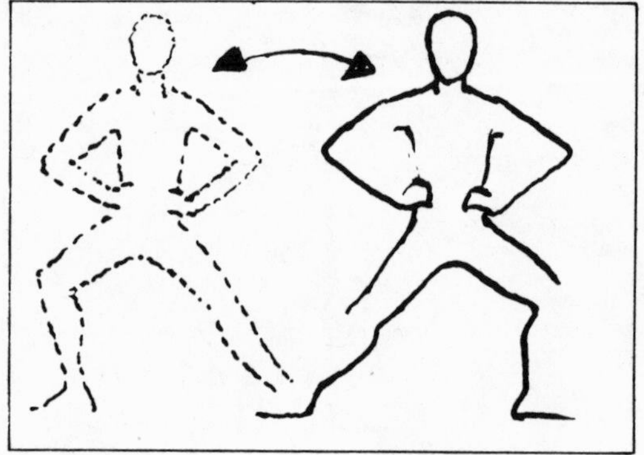

Exercise 2: Lower back and thigh

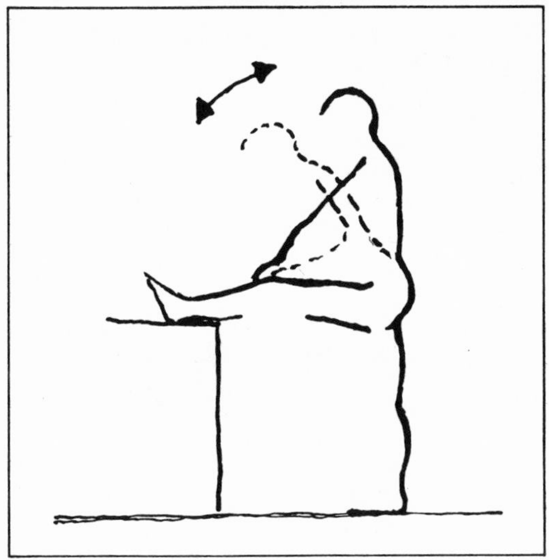

Exercise 3: Lower abdomen and front of thigh

Press hips forward with easy stretching, hands rest on forward knee, change forward leg at halfway point.

Exercise 4: Front of thigh

Hips forward, press heel up to buttocks.

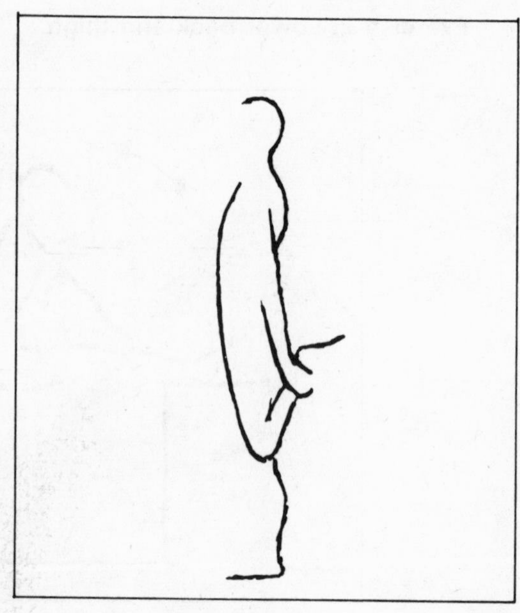

Exercise 5: Rear calf

Alternate bending, right and left ankle.

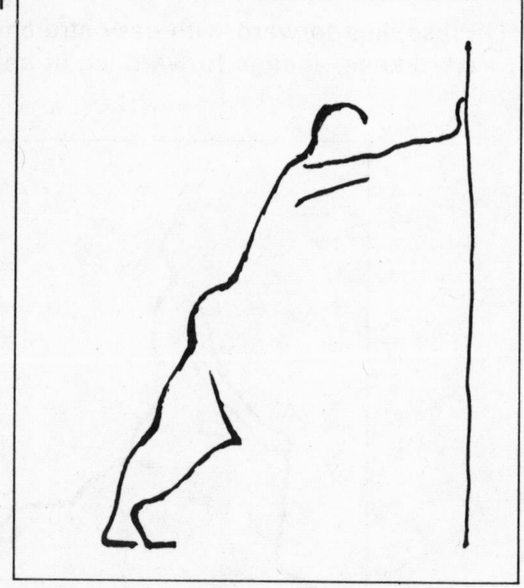

Exercise 6: Upper body

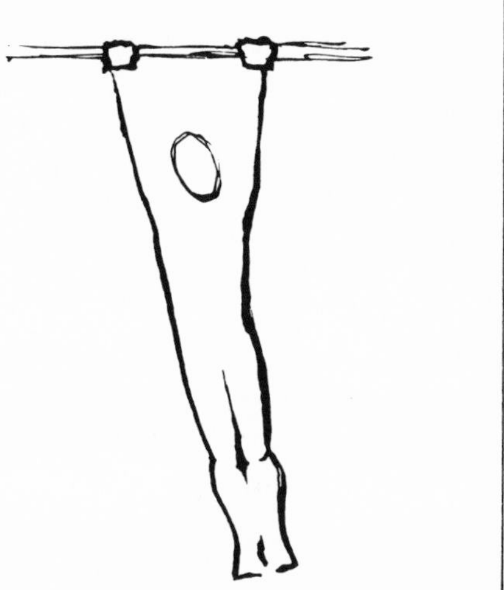

) Hang relaxed from overhead bar, swing lightly from side to side

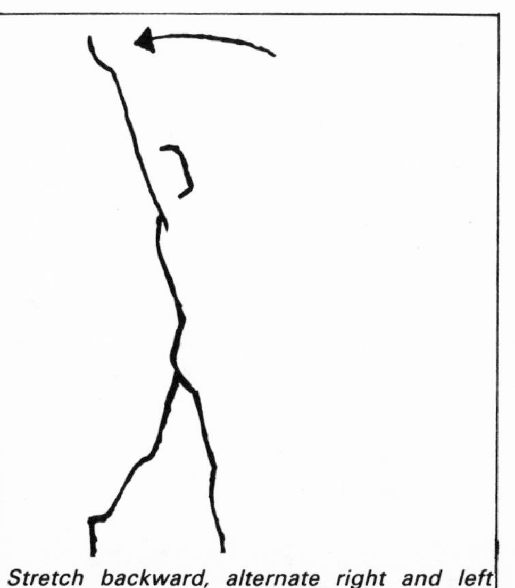

Stretch backward, alternate right and left forward

(c) Body bender from side to side

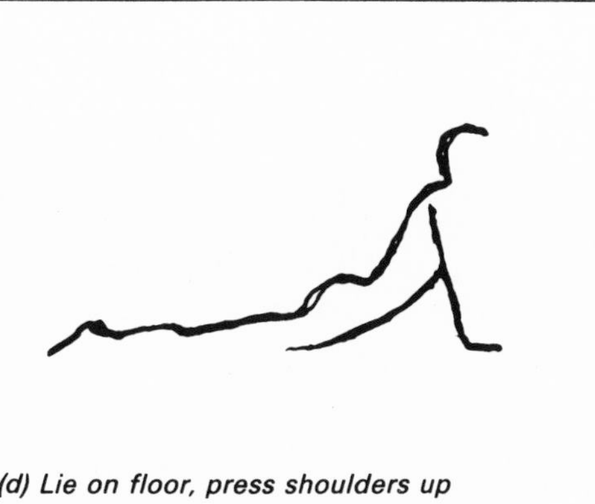

(d) Lie on floor, press shoulders up

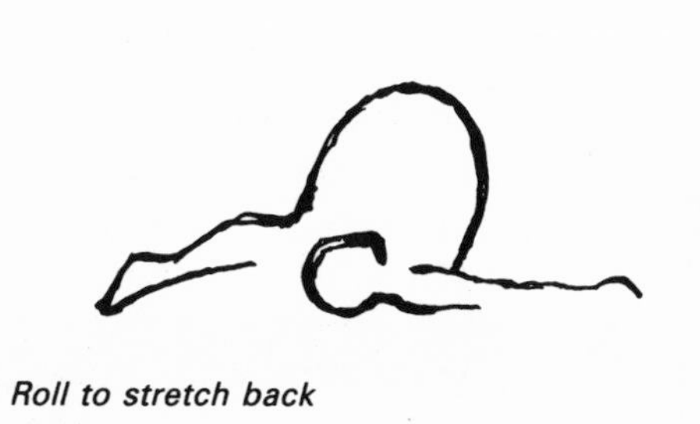

(e) Roll to stretch back

TECHNIQUE TRAINING

Generally you should be well rested and completely warmed up before you practice technique. However, experienced racers can work on technique even when tired.

Once the basics of technique are learned, you can combine endurance and technique training simply by trying to maintain "good style" throughout a whole tour. This type of technique training can be called "automatic" training—you practice a movement until it becomes automatic.

The most important time to work on technique is when you first get on skis at the start of the snow season. Some hints on how best to master the transition from foot to ski training are given in the following sample training programs.

THREE TYPICAL TRAINING PROGRAMS

No two skiers train exactly alike, but all should follow the general principles outlined in this chapter. However, individual programs can be set up following typical training programs for the major categories of skiers. Three such typical programs are presented here:

1. Program for boy and girl racers, 12 to 15 years old
2. Program for serious adult touring skiers
3. Program for adult active racers, women and men

The first and third categories cover most cross-country ski racers. The second may need some explanation. "Serious" adult touring skiers are defined as those who want to have the requisite fitness to do a lot of touring in any one season or to do well in tour races such as Sweden's Vasaloppet, or the Washington's Birthday Tour, Madonna Vasa, Gold Rush, or John Craig Memorial in the United States.

The three programs are written in abbreviated style using the various principles and exercises defined in this chapter. Endur-

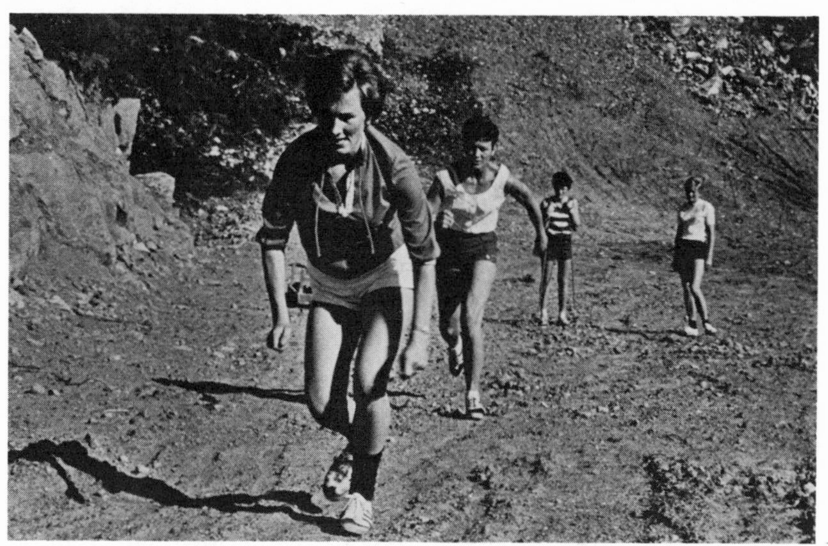

ance and technique training have been grouped together as best suits skiers.

All training periods should start with 10 to 15 minutes' warm-up (walking, jogging, easy skiing, easy stretching, etc.).

PROGRAM FOR BOY AND GIRL RACERS,
12 TO 15 YEARS OLD / September through February

Period	Endurance—Technique		Strength, Resilience, Speed	
	Periods per Week	Hours per Period	Periods per Week	Hours per Period
Off ski	3	½–1	1–2	½
Changeover to skiing	3	½–1¼	1	½
Competition	2–3 or 2 + 1 race	½–1¼	1	½

Older skiers should train more than younger. Fifteen-year-old boys should train using the maximum figures given, while both boys and girls twelve years old should use the minimum figures given.

Typical Weekly Program, Off Snow

1st day	Endurance training, walking, and running. Total time, ¾ to 1 hour.
2nd day	Rest.
3rd day	Strength and resilience training; total time, ½ hour.
4th day	Endurance training, walking, running, and ski striding. Total time, ½ to ¾ hour.
5th day	Rest, maybe 15 minutes' arm training.
6th day	Endurance training, running, walking, and ski striding. Total time, ¾ hour.
7th day	Rest.

Typical Weekly Program, Changeover to Skiing

1st day	Endurance and technique training: long, gentle uphills separated by flats and downhills. A good track is an advantage. Emphasize fluid, easy movement. Uphills should feel as tiring as on foot. Total time, ¾ to 1¼ hours.
2nd day	Rest, or a fun tour on skis.
3rd day	Technique, speed, resilience, and poling training. Vary between short, rapid sprints and long, easy "resting periods." Try to maintain good technique. Finish period with 6 to 7 minutes' diagonal stride on the flat. Total time, ½ to ¾ hour.
4th day	Endurance and technique training. Same as 1st day, but steeper hills, less total time.
5th day	Rest.
6th day	Endurance and technique training. Same as 1st day, but less total time, about ½ to ¾ hour total.
7th day	Rest, or a fun tour.

Typical Weekly Program, Racing Season

1st day	Race.
2nd day	Rest, easy jogging tour (on foot) or easy ski tour.
3rd day	Endurance and technique training. Stretch out on the flats and uphill. Total time, ¾ to 1¼ hours.
4th day	Rest, or fun tour.

5th day — Endurance and technique training, hilly terrain. Good speed on uphills. Total time, ½ to ¾ hour.

6th day — Technique, speed, resilience, and poling training. Vary between short, rapid sprints and long, easy "resting periods," both flats and uphills. Finish with 6 to 7 minutes' diagonal on the flat. Total time, ½ to ¾ hour.

7th day — Rest, or fun ski tour.

Not all twelve- and thirteen-year-olds can enjoy racing every week. "Rest Sundays" between racing Sundays are sometimes necessary.

SPRING AND SUMMER TRAINING Boys and girls need not concentrate specifically on cross-country training in the spring and summer months. They can easily maintain fitness by participating in other sports, by hiking, or by occasionally running in wooded areas.

PROGRAM FOR SERIOUS ADULT TOURING SKIERS / August through March

Period	Endurance—Technique		Strength, Resilience, Speed	
	Periods per Week	Hours per Period	Periods per Week	Hours per Period
Off ski	2	1–2½	1	¾
Changeover to skiing	3	1–3	1	½
Skiing	2 + 1 race	1–1		

Men should train using the maximum figures given, and women should train using the minimum figures given.

Typical Weekly Program, Off Snow

1st day — Endurance, distance training. Walking, ski striding, and running on soft surface. Total time, 1½ to 2½ hours.

2nd day	Rest.
3rd day	Strength and resilience training; total time, ¾ hour.
4th day	Rest.
5th day	Endurance, interval training. Walking, ski striding, and running in hilly terrain (or in a circular training course using a single uphill). Total time, 1 hour.
6th day	Rest.
7th day	Rest, or pole training; total time, 15 minutes.

Changeover to Snow

The first few tours should be short: excessively long tours can injure muscles unaccustomed to skiing. Use good tracks as much as possible. Try to ski easy and relaxed. Try to glide well but don't overdo gliding. Ski hills with power. Maintain endurance training throughout the changeover period. After 4 ski tours of about 1½ hours each, try the following program:

1st day	Endurance and technique, distance training. Easy tracks. Total time, 2 to 3 hours.
2nd day	Rest.
3rd day	Endurance and technique, natural interval training. Total time, 1 to 1½ hours.
4th day	Rest.
5th day	Technique, strength, resilience, and speed. Easy ski tours with occasional short, rapid sprints both on the flat and uphill. Finish with 10 minutes' double poling. Total time, 1½ hours.
6th day	Technique and endurance, easy distance training. Total time, 1½ hours.
7th day	Rest.

Typical Weekly Program, Tour Race Season

1st day	Tour race or Sunday tour.
2nd day	Rest.
3rd day	Technique and endurance, natural interval. Total time, 1 hour.
4th day	Rest.

5th day	Technique and endurance, distance training. Total time, 2 hours.
6th day	Rest.
7th day	Jogging tour on foot.

PROGRAM FOR ADULT ACTIVE RACERS / Year-round Training

Period	Endurance—Technique		Strength, Resilience, Speed	
	Periods per Week	Hours per Period[a]	Periods per Week	Hours per Period
Spring–summer "off season"	2	(1) [1½]	1–2	¾
Autumn "build-up"	4	(½–2) [1–3]	2	¾
Changeover to skiing	4–5	(1–2) [1–3]	1	¾
Competition	3–4 + 1–2 races	(1–2) [1–3]	1	¾

[a]Figures in parentheses are for women; figures in brackets are for men. All other figures in table are for both sexes. Junior men should use figures midway between those given for men and women.

"Off-Season" Training in Spring and Summer Months

Walking, ski striding, and running in hilly terrain twice a week with no special emphasis on cross-country. Total time: 1 hour per period for women, 1½ hours for men. Strength and resilience training once or twice a week, with primary emphasis on poling movements. If you have access to roller skis, use them.

Typical Weekly Program, Autumn "Build-up" Period

1st day	Endurance, distance training. Walking, ski striding, and running on a soft surface. Total time: 2 hours for women, 3 hours for men.
2nd day	Strength and resilience training, if possible roller ski training. Total time, ¾ hour.
3rd day	Endurance, distance training. Walking, ski striding, and running in rugged terrain. Total time: 1½ hours for women, 2 hours for men.

4th day Rest.

5th day Endurance, interval training. Ski stride and bounding ski stride with poles, up and down a single hill or in a circular, hilly training course. Total time: ¾ hour for women, 1 hour for men.

6th day Strength training, poling movements, if possible on roller skis; total time, ½ hour. Followed by a short but hard running tour. Finish with a tempo sprint. Total time, 1 to 1½ hours.

7th day Rest.

Typical Weekly Program, Changeover to Skiing

The first few tours should be short; excessively long tours can injure muscles unaccustomed to skiing. Use good tracks as much as possible. Try to ski easy and relaxed. Try to glide well but don't overdo gliding. Ski hills with power. Maintain endurance training throughout the changeover period. After 4 ski tours of about 1½ hours each for women and 2 hours each for men, try the following program:

1st day Endurance and technique, distance training. Easy track. Total time: 2 hours for women, 3 hours for men.

2nd day Endurance and technique, distance training. Total time: 1½ hours for women, 2 hours for men.

3rd day Endurance and technique, natural interval. Total time: 1 hour for women, 1½ hours for men.

4th day Rest.

5th day Technique, strength, resilience, and speed. Easy ski tours with occasional short, rapid sprints both on the flat and uphill. Finish with 10 minutes' double poling. Total time, 1½ hours.

6th day Endurance and technique, natural interval. Finish with a couple of tempo sprints. Total time: 1 hour for women, 1½ hours for men.

7th day Rest, or perhaps a relaxing ski tour concentrating on fine points of technique, such as downhill and turning.

Junior girls following this program should always have two rest days per week.

Typical Weekly Program, Competition Season

1st day	Race.
2nd day	Rest, or easy distance training. Total time: 1 ½ hours for women, 2 hours for men.
3rd day	Endurance and technique, natural interval in hilly terrain. Total time: 1 hour for women, 1 ½ hours for men.
4th day	Race or tempo training. Long rests between tempo sprints. Keep moving in rests, perfecting technique. Total time, 1 hour.
5th day	Endurance and technique, distance training. Total time: 2 hours for women, 2 to 3 hours for men.
6th day	Endurance and technique, natural interval. Finish with 10 minutes double poling. Total time: 1 hour for women, 1 ½ hours for men.
7th day	Rest, or a short jogging tour on foot.

After the race season, it's best to stop training according to a fixed program. Just ski 3 or 4 tours per week, concentrating on technique and experimenting with different forms of training.

TRAINING TESTING

Endurance and Strength Tests The true test of effective training is improved skiing times. But it's also useful to have some sort of check on whether or not endurance or strength increase with training. In testing, it's best to check only one capability at a time: for instance, a test for aerobic endurance, a test for anaerobic endurance, and tests for strengths of the various muscle groups.

Tests are best run during the autumn build-up period, but are also useful before training starts as an indication of the weaknesses on which training should concentrate.

The test methods described in this book are chiefly used to test individual fitness from month to month or from year to year.

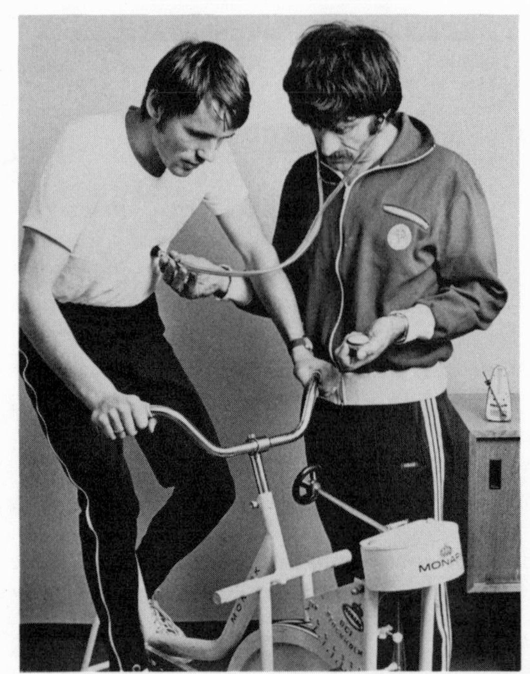

Above: Ergometer cycle test
Below: Equipment for Ergometer cycle test

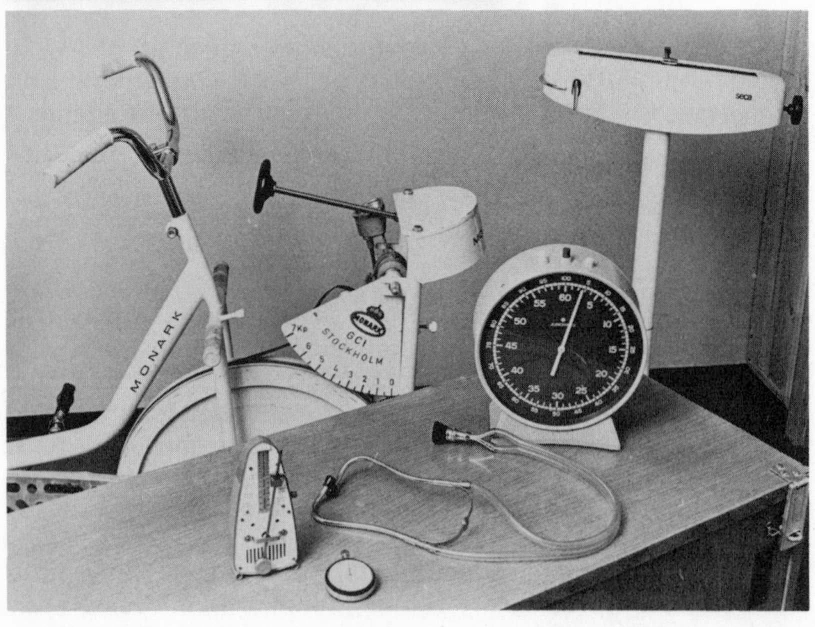

They can also be used to compare skiers, but such comparisons should not be taken as absolute indications of individual performance. Monthly training testing is recommended for racers who want a regular training check.

Endurance Tests

Measuring Aerobic Endurance Maximum oxygen uptake is one of the factors contributing to maximum aerobic capacity, which, in turn, is a major factor in endurance. Maximum oxygen uptake is best measured by direct methods such as running on a treadmill or pedaling an Ergometer cycle for a period of time in which expelled air is collected and analyzed for oxygen content. The direct methods are accurate, but can be performed only in physiological laboratories.

The indirect Ergometer cycle test has become almost the standard test, for it is one of the most reliable and most easily administered. In the indirect Ergometer test, the subject pedals a stationary cycle at a constant speed against a fixed resistance for a period of about 6 minutes. The pulse rate is taken at 1-minute intervals, and the test is regarded as finished when the pulse rate is stable, which usually is between the 4th and 6th minute. This information, combined with the subject's maximum heart rate and information on body weight, sex, and age, gives maximum oxygen uptake.

The test is best used as an index of individual training progress. It is most easily interpreted if the subject pedals against the same resistance at the same speed every month. A lowered pulse from month to month indicates progress.

The *step test,* an outgrowth of the army "pack test" and Harvard step test, indicates aerobic capacity. The subject stands with feet together beside a platform or bench about 16 inches high (for trained adults). He first steps up with one leg and then the other to assume a full standing position on the platform. This is followed by a step down, starting with the leg first used, and then the other leg. This is continued for 5 minutes at an even pace, usually 30 times per minute. The pulse rate is taken at predetermined periods (usually 30 seconds) after stepping stops. Lowered pulse from test to test indicates increased aerobic capacity. Test loads can be varied by using higher steps or by increasing step frequency. Testing can be interpreted in many ways, including taking pulse rates at half-minute intervals after stepping to determine the pulse recovery rate. It is, of course, most important to keep the conditions the same from test to test so results may be compared. Step heights should be 16 inches for trained adults, 12 inches for boys and girls, and about 8 to 10 inches for untrained subjects. The step test is not as accurate as the Ergometer test and it can be influenced by psychological disturbances.

Rest pulse rate can indicate level of training or fitness. If measured regularly over a period of several months, a diminishing rest pulse can indicate increasing endurance capability.

However, many physiologists believe that it is extremely difficult to truly measure the rest pulse, if the rest pulse can be defined at all. The pulse rate of a person at rest can be influenced by many external factors including psychological ones. Pulse rates increase when eyes open, when voices are heard nearby, or when the senses register a disturbance.

TEST TRACKS Running time over a fixed distance on a fixed path of about 10 minutes' duration can be used as a test of endurance. Pick a path or trail with a solid, even base and a continuous but slight (3- to 7-degree) uphill. Steeper uphills are unadvisable, as it is then difficult to maintain a constant tempo for more than 2 to 3 minutes. Run the distance and record your times; lowered times mean better endurance. But be sure that the test conditions are as constant as possible. The path shouldn't be slippery for one test and dry for another, nor should you test on the coldest autumn day or warmest summer day. Try to wear the same shoes and clothes for all tests.

Measuring Anaerobic Endurance Anaerobic endurance or anaerobic capacity is a measure of the body's capability to perform short-term muscular work over and above the limit set by maximum oxygen uptake. Thus the amount of anaerobic work performed is often measured as "oxygen debt," with a high oxygen debt indicating a high anaerobic capacity. The anaerobic process involves a breakdown of glucose into lactic acid. The amount of this process that occurs is also a measure of anaerobic capacity. Neither oxygen debt nor lactic acid level is easily measured; only a few physiological laboratories are equipped to make these tests.

The best method of testing anaerobic capacity for all practical purposes is testing by running sprints.

TEST SPRINTS High exercise loads of duration up to one minute chiefly depend on the anaerobic processes. Therefore improvement on short stretches up to 1 minute in duration is an indication of improved anaerobic capacity.

Pick a slight (3- to 7-degree grade) hill for running or a slightly steeper (about 15-degree grade) hill for bounding ski stride with poles. Test as follows: After a thorough warm-up, run the distance at maximum speed, taking your time. Rest for 4 minutes, and then run again. Compare times from month to month, from year to year.

Testing Muscle Strength and Resilience/Speed

Maximum muscle strength is simply measured as the maximum load a muscle can lift, pull, or push. Repetitive muscle strength is of greater interest in cross-country.

MEASURING REPETITIVE MUSCLE STRENGTH Repetitive muscle strength has the broad definition of being a muscle or muscle group's ability to overcome a given resistance a large number of times in succession.

For a cross-country skier, repetitive muscle strength is best measured by providing a load that can be overcome at least 10 to 50 times in the first test. Untrained persons often increase their repetitive muscle strength so rapidly during systematic training that their second test will show improvements in overcoming the same resistance of up to 100 times or more. In such cases, the loads should be increased.

Suggested Exercises for Testing Repetitive Muscle Strength for Cross-country Racers The tests should involve the muscle groups most used in cross-country and should be in movements like those used in cross-country technique. Body positions and movements as well as tempo should be the same from test to test, as the maximum number of repetitions are usually what is counted as a test result.

SQUAT TEST With load on shoulders, squat to position where thighs are parallel to floor, and then straighten up, as illustrated at the top of the next page. Count maximum number of squats.

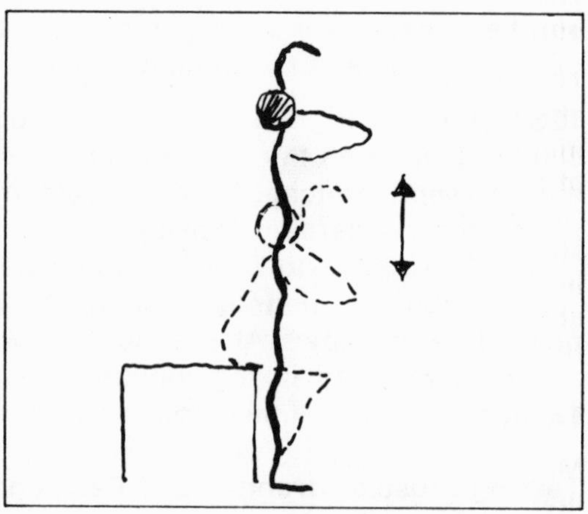

Squat test, down to position with thighs almost horizontal.

POLING MOVEMENTS Arm-training apparatus can be used for testing repetitive arm strength. Simply continue arm exercises until a maximum is reached, and note the maximum. The same method can be used for the other muscle groups using the exercises described on pages 142–147.

Measuring Resilience and Speed/BOUNDING SKI STRIDE WITHOUT POLES Take time (about 10 seconds) for bounding ski stride up a fixed hill over a fixed distance. Take average of two runs with a 2-minute rest between runs.

BOUNDING SKI STRIDE WITH POLES Same sequence as bounding ski stride without poles.

Choice of Tests For a cross-country skier, endurance is most important and maximum muscle strength least important, although these two qualities do depend somewhat on each other. All things being equal, the order of importance of testing for cross-country skiing is:

1 endurance skiing

2 repetitive muscle-strength testing

3 resilience/speed testing

4 maximum strength testing

6

Racing Hints

Start of the 4 × 10 km relay in the 1974 FIS Nordic World Ski Championships, won by East Germany.

6

Racing Hints

Athleticism must be, and should be, adult "play." It is when we make it work—dull, routined, scheduled, treadmill work—that we depart from the natural, the joyous, the exhilarating.
Percy Wells Cerutty, *Athletics, How to Become a Champion*

"Strong man of . . . ," "wonder girl . . ." Athletes apparently capable of exceeding themselves are often described by press and public as if they were superhuman. It's really more a question of experience, judgment, concentration, and will. Both experience and judgment increase with competition. Concentration and will can be learned; psychological training is the most valuable form of training one gets in racing.

This chapter offers no prescription, no shortcut to better racing. It simply offers useful hints to *successful* racing.

DAY BEFORE THE RACE

CHECK YOUR EQUIPMENT If you have wood-base skis, check and perhaps scrape the bottoms, warm in tar, or base binder wax. If there's a possibility of new snow or wind pack in the track, don't tar skis the day before.

Check your bindings and tighten loose screws. Check pole shafts, baskets, and wrist loops.

TRAINING AND REST Before minor races, especially early in the season, train as usual with no more rest than you would take before a normal training day. But remember that races are really hard training which can rob you of excess ability to perform. Don't add races to the training that you normally follow, but rather let them replace some training periods. A shorter race can be regarded as a mixture of aerobic and anaerobic training. A long race, such as a 30- or 50-km race for men, is really an overdose of aerobic training. In other words, a men's 30-km race is like two hours' constant interval training.

Most racers should train less and more easily than usual the last 3 to 4 days before a major race. Some racers find that a short jogging tour on foot is adequate for the last 2 days before a race.

Rest and relaxation are important, both between longer training periods and between demanding races. Some racers can't do without sleep, while others seem to race well even after a sleepless night. As a general rule, however, several days of lost sleep and relaxation decrease ability in endurance events. But it's chiefly a personal thing; individual differences determine just how well you do with or without sleep. Don't feel whipped before a start if you have tossed and turned instead of sleeping the night before.

"Charging Up"

For a racer, getting "charged up" for a race involves both psychological and physical preparation.

Psychological "charging up" means that you have a good balance between relaxation and concentration. Before an important race you should have more than adequate time to relax and sleep, but you should also want to race, to measure yourself against your competitors.

Physical "charging up" involves both physiological factors such as adequate rest to recover from previous races or training, and good nutrition.

If you've been training hard for some time, your overall fitness can actually increase as you rest for a couple of days to recover from training. Fitness progress sometimes lags training.

A normal balanced diet is usually adequate for a cross-country racer, regardless of the amount and intensity of training. Some endurance-event coaches favor iron supplements in a training diet. It has often been shown that endurance training decreases the iron content in the blood, but it is not universally accepted whether or not such a decrease is a natural circulatory system reaction or if it poses a threat to increased aerobic endurance.

You can stockpile for longer races (1½ hours or more) by eating larger quantities of carbohydrates and less fat and proteins for a few days before the race. Bread, potatoes, vegetables, and sweets are thus "stockpiling food." Furthermore, take in adequate liquids the day and evening before a race. Simply drink until you are no longer thirsty, but no more.

Other, more physiologically involved, methods of stockpiling have been used in Scandinavian racing circles. Two such methods are as follows.

1. Train hard for 3 hours or more approximately 4 days before an important race. The idea is to exercise until the body is completely "empty." Then eat a diet having high carbohydrate content but little fat or protein the remaining days before the race. Liquid intake should be normal.

2. Hard training or a long race 6 or 7 days before an important race. Then go on a 2- to 3-day diet of chiefly proteins and fats such as fish, meat, and eggs. Then a hard training day such that the body is "completely empty." Then a high-carbohydrate, low-fat or protein diet until the race. Liquid intake should be normal.

The second method is regarded as more effective than the first, but it is also more complicated and more difficult to follow in practice, chiefly because it disrupts training. In addition, it may be monotonous to eat the same sort of food for 3 days.

Carbohydrate stockpiling is important because carbohydrates are stored as glucose in the muscles to become the fuel for extended work such as cross-country racing. The normal glucose reserves are limited to cover only 1½ to 2 hours' hard skiing.

When muscular glucose is expended, it can be replenished by a "refill" provided the refilling is done soon after the emptying; for example, by "stockpiling" as described above.

Dehydration—Liquid Deficiency in the Body

The body should have an adequate liquid (water) content the day before a race. Liquid deficiency—dehydration—can occur quickly in cross-country racing, usually after 50 minutes' skiing.

HOURS BEFORE THE START

DIET AND "CHARGING UP" Normally, if races start early in the day, a single meal before a race is adequate. It should be easily digestible and comprise chiefly carbohydrates but little protein or fats. Take in liquids. Some skiers prefer skim milk, while others prefer tea, coffee, or fruit juices. Sour milk is more easily digested than sweet milk. Half an hour to an hour before a start of a 30- to 50-km race, take in extra liquids in the form of juices or tea with sugar.

Normally, you should stop stockpiling at least 2 to 3 hours before a start. Some racers can nibble almost up to the start, however; for many, such eating is relaxing.

Psychological readiness is the most important in prerace hours.

Avoid irritation; the "devil-may-care" attitude often wins.

Systematic preparation keeps you calm. Allow plenty of time to get your number, check your clothing and equipment, and test your wax.

Look forward to the race. You have everything to win, nothing to lose. A nonwin in a race is no shame.

Don't fear your competitors. Try to relax completely for 15 minutes before warm-up. Normally you can be finished with waxing and testing your skis an hour before the start. Sometimes you may have to wax and test wax almost until you start. But don't feel that you've lost if you don't rest before warming up. You're never the only one with problems before a race.

Testing Wax

Test skis where the snow is well tracked and clean. Hard waxes are usually better after they've been skied on a bit, but klisters wear with use. For heavy corn snow or icy tracks, it's best to warm up on a pair of training skis or warm up on foot.

Warming Up

Warming up before a race is important. In many cases it is more important than precise waxing or resting before a start. Warm up for 20 to 30 minutes before a race, but a little less before a long race.

WHILE RACING

DISTRIBUTE YOUR RESOURCES It's almost always best to start easy, even though you are well warmed up. The poorer your fitness, the less you can tolerate a hard start.

You usually get into an oxygen debt at a start; the harder the start, the greater the debt. This debt often results in muscular stiffness, sore throat, or nausea. The seconds gained in a hard start are more than doubly lost later when you have to "pay back" an oxygen debt. On the other hand, if you start easily, you can push harder as you get the feel of the race.

At the end of a race, just go for all you're worth—you can more than gain back seconds lost in an easy start.

Liquids, Sugar, and Nourishment in Longer Races

After an hour's racing, an adult racer has lost at least a quart of liquid. This amounts to a 5 to 10 percent reduction of work capacity.

After 3 hours' hard skiing, liquid loss can run from 3 to 4 quarts, and work capacity is reduced to less than 70 percent of its "normal" level.

These losses of work capacity because of liquid loss mean that liquids must be consumed in races lasting 1 to 1½ hours or more.

Liquid loss reduces performance before the lack of muscular glucose is felt. Thus liquid replacement is primary. But since glucose reserves can be depleted, it is necessary to take in glucose for races lasting 1½ hours or more.

Common opinion holds that salt should be taken in if you sweat profusely. This is not always so. The salt concentration in body fluids is three times as great as that in sweat, which means that if you sweat a lot, your bodily salt level increases unless you take in liquids. In practice, it is almost impossible for a cross-country racer, even in a 30-km or 50-km race, to take in so much liquid that his bodily salt level decreases. Therefore it is doubtful if taking in salt has any benefit in races lasting less than 3 or 4 hours.

For races of 1½ hours or more, physiological testing and racing experience indicate that one to two cups of liquid per 5 km of race are needed, with the first "feeding" after the first 5 km.

Feeding liquids should:

—contain about 5 to 10 percent sugar by weight, slightly more in extremely cold weather

—be about body temperature

—be slightly tasty (fruit juice additives with a little salt are fine)

Feeding liquids should not be strongly sweet or salty.

Rewaxing

Rewaxing is seldom helpful in races lasting an hour or less. However, rewaxing in 50-km or longer tour races often helps overall time.

Icing: Waxing icy skis in a hurry is almost impossible. If your skis ice up, simply scrape both ice and wax off and rewax. If the icing is due to water penetrating the skis, there is little you can do in a race without a waxing torch to dry out your skis.

Slippery skis can be made to bite by waxing softer wax in the middle of the camber.

AFTER A RACE

Drink, Food, and Talking

Common opinion has held that you should drink something warm after a hard race, basically to prevent colds and other respiratory infections. Such drinks have been served after both short and long races. But if you think back to the finish of a race, you'll remember that you don't feel like drinking much. Anything warmer than body temperature is more unpleasant than helpful. Overwarm drinks gulped down while you are out of breath can burn your throat and, in fact, make you more susceptible to infection.

After long races of 1½ hours' duration or more, drink only small portions of body-temperature drinks. Avoid ice-cold drinks —but if you can't resist a cold drink, take it in small portions.

Postrace drinks should contain glucose, such as fruit juice, sugared tea or water, or warm soft drinks.

Racers seldom have an appetite right after a race. This is no indication of sickness, it's usual; the body isn't ready to take in solid food after hard muscular work. Wait an hour or two to eat something easily digestible. Eat a late dinner on race days.

Just after a finish you're probably out of breath and feel a slight hoarseness in your throat. Don't overload your throat by talking—at least not for 15 minutes or so. Let your throat recover from all the cold-air pumping it has been doing before you talk too much.

Bath

Take a warm bath or shower and change into dry clothes as soon as possible after a finish. After a hard race you are more than usually susceptible to viral sicknesses such as colds and influenza. Furthermore, muscles that have worked hard in a race can be sensitive and hurt if they cool down quickly after the finish; a minor strain can then become a major pain.

Sportsmanship

It's enjoyable to win and sad to lose. Those who win or lose must be allowed to show their feelings without being regarded as unsportsmanlike. But some human restraint is in order; a winner should not be a show-off even if he has won many times. A loser shouldn't try to find a scapegoat in his competitors; he should take his loss in a way that doesn't irritate others.

7
Instruction

7
Instruction

Many good cross-country racers and proficient touring skiers have never had a single hour's instruction. Most of them started ski touring as children, and then learned by watching and mimicking good skiers. But most of all, they have done a lot of skiing.

This doesn't mean that ski-touring instruction is unnecessary. True, the movements of touring are very much like walking and thus most people are equipped with a modicum of touring knowledge even if they have never skied. But touring movements are different enough from walking and normal on-foot activity so as to require explanation, and thus instruction.

Even some of the more proficient cross-country racers and touring skiers would be still better had they had instruction at an early stage. And then there are many less proficient skiers and beginners who haven't had the advantage of growing up on skis. They all can be better skiers by taking ski lessons.

In touring and cross-country "terrain is the best teacher" to the extent that the preparation and arrangement of instruction are often more important than the particular technique of instruction itself. Specifically:

—Ski equipment must be in good working order and of a type suited to the pupils' needs and proficiency.

—Skis should be waxed for the day's conditions.

—The instruction area and tracks should be prepared and should suit the pupils' proficiency.

"Practice makes perfect" is another touring and cross-country instructional maxim. The class line-up, all too common in Alpine ski instruction, has no place in touring and cross-country instruction. Pupils should move as much as possible, practicing their skills in varying terrain.

INSTRUCTION AREA AND TRACKS

Instruction is usually done on parallel tracks, closed-loop courses, or on longer tours. Parallel tracks are usually used for beginners or for practice of a single movement. Closed-loop courses keep pupils moving, provide terrain variation, and drill in movements learned on parallel tracks. Longer tours for instructional purposes usually combine technique instruction with endurance training for advanced touring skiers or cross-country racers.

Tracks should be prepared in advance for parallel-track and closed-loop instruction. For adult instruction, the tracks should be set such that with skis parallel and in the tracks, the distance between the inside edges of the right and left binding ears is 5 to 6 inches. For children's instruction, the corresponding distance should be 4 to 5 inches.

Parallel tracks on the flat should be 75 to 200 yards long, one track for each pupil, 2 yards between tracks. The instructor's demonstration track should cut across the pupils' tracks 10 to 20 yards from one end.

Parallel-track instruction with instructor's track cut across pupils' tracks.

Closed-loop instruction track may be laid out around a parallel-track area.

Short loop course should be 700 to 1,000 yards long, on the flat or in varying terrain as needed. Avoid dips and sharp turns for beginners. Extra tracks can be added to the main track for special purposes such as passing, individual practice, etc. The instructor may either check a single movement by standing at one place, or check all movements by skiing around the course, preferably outside the main track in the direction opposite to that of the pupils.

Parallel tracks uphill: Used for group instruction of uphill technique. Here the instructor can't have a separate crossing track, but must ski in one of the uphill tracks. Pupils can stop, turn, and ski downhill in the same tracks.

Up-down loops: Better for large groups than parallel tracks uphill. Two or three uphill tracks according to need. Lay out tracks so that there's no uphill waiting. Pupils ski to right or left at top and then ski downhill in tracks parallel to the uphill tracks.

Up-down instruction loops should be laid out so that there is no waiting for uphill skiing.

Long loops should be 2 to 5 miles long for combining instruction with endurance training for advanced touring skiers and cross-country racers. They should be laid out in such a way that the loop has a couple of flat sections, a couple of easy uphills, one or two steeper uphills, at least one short, steep uphill where pupils must herringbone, and one to three downhills. The downhills should be free of trees and shrubs, stumps, stones or other obstructions so that the pupils can free ski, turning at will.

Technique on tours: Good racers and touring skiers usually work on technique on the season's first few, longer ski tours.

ORGANIZATION OF CLASSES

Small classes are most effective; seven to eight pupils is ideal. An instructor should usually have no more than fifteen pupils. If an instructor is alone with a class of twenty or more pupils, then it's best to divide the class in two. Start with a short instruction period for both halves, then send one half out to practice on a loop while the other half gets specific instruction. Change groups every 20 to 30 minutes.

Pupils' understanding is vital. The instructor must stand and move so that all pupils can see and hear him. For technique instruction, such as in parallel tracks, the pupils should *not* stand with a glaring sun or blowing snow directly in their faces. It's best to demonstrate every movement twice so that the pupils can view it from at least two angles (for instance; diagonal stride from the side and front).

Practice makes perfect for the pupils. Avoid excessive talk and demonstration; passive pupils don't learn. Keep them moving.

Correcting mistakes can be helpful if done positively. But it's more important to tell a pupil what to do to correct a mistake.

TEACHING BEGINNERS TECHNIQUE

There are several methods of teaching cross-country and touring technique. The simplest method involves imitation: The instructor demonstrates a movement, and the pupils learn by imitation, trial, and error, with very little correction from the instructor. This is the *mimic method;* it is simple, yet effective. It is especially suitable for teaching children.

The *"whole method"* is perhaps the most often used in cross-country and touring instruction. It resembles the *mimic method* in that the pupils always perform a whole movement. But it differs in that it involves a sequence of demonstration, trial, explanation, and correction:

1. The instructor briefly describes and then demonstrates a whole movement.
2. The pupils attempt and briefly practice.
3. The instructor comments on common errors to the whole class and then corrects individual errors by assigning individual tasks (corrective movements).

The instructor should systematically go through the different components of a whole movement, but should never pick it apart until it is only a series of components. For instance, in teaching the diagonal stride to beginners, the instructor lets the pupils start with the whole movement, but emphasizes diagonal movement and rhythm in all initial comments and corrections. Once the pupils are more proficient in these two components, the instructor shifts emphasis to leg work, and then to body position and arm work. Finally, when all components seem correct, the instructor reemphasizes the stride as a whole.

The *"part method"* is sometimes useful. It involves instruction in and practice of a single component of a finished movement. For instance, pupils having difficulty coordinating arm-leg movements in the diagonal stride are usually simply confused by their poles. Letting them ski for a while without poles will build confidence and restore their natural arm-leg coordination. This exercise in part of a final movement is useful, but should be limited so that the pupils concentrate on the whole movement and not its individual parts. For instance, pupils who ski too much without poles may have difficulty learning a good body position and arm movements for the diagonal stride. This is because 25 percent or more of the body's forward drive and side-to-side balance in the diagonal stride come from the arms. Skiing without poles removes this balance and drive and thus can actually teach incorrect diagonal striding if carried to extremes. Pupils should not ski without poles for more than 15 to 20 minutes at a stretch.

In some cases, one complete movement can be regarded as a part of another complete movement. For instance, straight double poling should be taught before the double-pole stride, and the flat-terrain skating turn should be taught before the downhill skating turn.

However, the whole method is generally preferable to the part method in teaching cross-country and touring technique. Movements such as arm-swing in place, kicking in place, etc., should be used only in extreme cases as corrective movements and should never be more than brief pauses in lessons otherwise emphasizing whole movements.

Progression

Progression simply means going from the easy to the more difficult. In learning the diagonal stride it means starting with short, walklike strides and short glides and progressing to more powerful kicks and longer glides. It also means starting in easier terrain, such as on the flat, and working up to more difficult terrain, such as a loop track in varying terrain.

CORRECTING MISTAKES

Spotting and correcting mistakes is an instructor's most important job. Five important rules for successful correction are:

1. Correct only one mistake at a time.
2. Correct each mistake with a single corrective task for the pupil to perform.

3. Correct the most important mistakes first. Minor fine points of lesser significance for efficiency of movement should be corrected last.
4. An instructor shouldn't measure his ability by seeing how many mistakes he can spot at once. It's far better to say too little and correct too few mistakes than to overwhelm the pupil with an avalanche of corrections.
5. Be certain that a mistake is really a mistake before correcting. Pupils must be allowed individual style suiting their body type and general physical condition. It's wrong for an instructor to try to make all pupils ski exactly alike.

SPECIFIC INSTRUCTION

Diagonal Stride

The diagonal stride is used far more than any other movement in ski touring and cross-country racing. Diagonal movements are also used in changing strides in varying terrain. These facts, together with the natural simplicity of the stride, mean that the diagonal stride should be the first taught and the most practiced.

The diagonal stride is actually a bit easier to do correctly up a slight incline than on the flat. Some instructors prefer to start diagonal stride instruction up a slight incline for just this reason, while others feel that flat terrain is better for beginners. From a pure instructional point of view, there's very little difference between a flat and a slight incline, so the choice between the two is purely a matter of preference on the part of the instructor. In any case, the pupils should have tracks long enough to allow them time to fall into a rhythmic movement pattern.

Some amateur instructors, realizing that the glide is the chief difference between diagonal on foot and diagonal on skis, emphasize gliding when instructing beginners. This is a serious error. Overemphasizing the glide can introduce staccato rhythm and destroy arm-leg coordination. The glide will come naturally as pupils gain balance and rhythm.

Good instruction should always build on the pupils' previous knowledge and capabilities. All pupils know how to walk, so the simplest progression starts with walking. First, have the pupils walk without poles just as if they were walking on foot. Try to get them to relax and forget the skis on their feet. Their shoulders and arms should be relaxed; arms should swing freely forward and back. "Pushing-off" (kicking) a bit harder will automatically introduce shorter glides. Then a bit of a forward body lean from the waist and slightly harder kicks increase glide length.

Poleless skiing should be used only as a transition between the pupils' natural walking abilities and the desired skiing diagonal stride. As soon as possible, and preferably after the first 15 minutes of beginning "ski walking," the pupils should start skiing with poles. If a pupil's movements become staccato or lacking in arm-leg coordination, however, shorter periods of poleless diagonal striding can be used to build coordination and rhythm.

Many adult pupils and almost all children find practicing strides a bit monotonous. Good instruction provides variety to hold interest. But beginning students are not proficient enough to go on a tour or seek variety through different skiing exercises. So in the beginning, games are helpful, especially with children. Try, for instance:

"Who can glide the longest on one ski?"

"Who skis from here to there with the fewest kicks?"

"First man to the other end of the tracks wins."

"Skate a little—with free-swinging arms."

These games are excellent balance exercises and, more important, help reduce the pupils' feelings of awkwardness on skis. But, like poleless diagonal skiing, they must be short because in excess they can impair learning of correct diagonal rhythm with poles.

Uphill Diagonal Stride

Use packed firm tracks going from a flat up a gradually increasing incline.

To maintain speed, tempo must increase as the incline gets steeper and glides get shorter. The most common mistake made is for pupils to get into a frenzy of arm and leg movements and thus lose their flat diagonal technique. Corrective tasks such as "try to keep your speed with stronger kicks," "weight on one ski at a time," or "pole a bit stronger with your arms bent a bit more" counteract the pupils' natural tendency to scramble as soon as they feel they might slip.

As soon as the pupils seem to ski well up a slight incline, they can start on uphill traversing and herringbone.

Double Poling

Beginners should first try double poling on a slight downhill or on the flat if snow conditions are good. The practice tracks should be long enough for the pupils to get up enough speed to do several double polings, and the sides of the tracks should be well packed to provide a good bite for the poles. The slope of the tracks should be selected according to the pupils' physical condition. If the resistance to overcome is too great with respect to their arm strength, they may easily get into a sitting position in double poling, which is a bad start.

Instruction in double poling should start with strideless, straight double poling. For instruction, the important components of the movement are:

Weight well over poles and pull with arms bent.

Push backward with loosening grip and arms straightening.

Knees bend during double poling, but *don't sit!*

Poling should be strong enough and speed should be great enough so that the pupils have enough time to straighten up to an almost erect position between polings. If not, practice on a steeper downhill track.

Start teaching the double-pole stride as soon as the pupils seem to have grasped the essentials of strideless double poling. This usually happens after about a quarter of an hour's practice. Concentrate on increasing double-poling power and rapidity and strength of kicks between successive double polings.

As with the diagonal stride, the major criterion for judging successful double poling is simply whether or not the pupils have relaxed, easy movements that push them forward efficiently.

Changing Strides

Instruction in changing strides should not be taken up as a separate subject, but rather should be fitted naturally into instruction in other strides as soon as the pupils have mastered the fundamentals of the diagonal stride and double poling. The chief things to watch for are unnecessary movements and unusually long breaks in rhythm.

Step Turn and Skating Turn

The step turn and the skating turn are related and should be taught in the same lesson, with the step turn being first. Snow should be firmly packed for both the kick and the double poling of the skating turn; the step turn can be done in looser snow.

Although skating turns are usually made in a track in many tours and in almost all races, it's best to start instruction on a firm, untracked snow surface. In this manner the pupils are not constrained to a fixed movement and can gradually build up their capability.

Start with poleless turns and work up to the use of poles, going from the step turn to the skating turn:

Practice without poles:

Step turn on a slight downhill

Skating turn on the flat, to the right and to the left, with a little speed from a slight downhill

Skating turn in a single direction, with arm swing

Skating turn around a bush, tree, or pole in the snow

Practice with poles:

Skating turn initiated with double poling

Skating turn initiated and finished with double poling

Skating turn, one side only

Skating turn, alternating left and right

Games helpful in instruction:

Mimic skaters

Poleless skating turns through a slalom course of poles set up on the flat

Steeper Uphill Technique

The chief rule for instruction in steeper uphill technique is to keep it short; it just isn't fun for beginners. Change and vary, throwing in a bit of easier uphill and downhill instruction.

For beginners, tacking turns are best taught using the mimic method. Simply demonstrate the different tacking turns and let the pupils themselves discover the easiest way of getting over the fall-line. More advanced pupils with difficulties in uphill tacking turns can be taught the parts of the turns in more detail. Pupils should never be taught a fixed tacking turn, as the various component movements of the turn should always be altered to suit the skier's speed, snow conditions, and steepness of hill.

The herringbone should be taught when the pupils seem ready to learn or need the stride.

The most common mistake to watch for in uphill traversing, tacking turns, and herringbone is that pupils sometimes try to take small uphill steps on their toes—as if they were kicking their feet into the hard snow surface. This is perhaps one of the few natural on-foot movements that must be counteracted in teaching touring technique. In all uphill technique, body weight should be well on the kicking foot to avoid skis slipping back downhill. The next most common mistake is that some pupils tend to hang on their poles, as if pulling themselves uphill by gripping a banister. This natural reaction from on-foot movement must also be counteracted. The uphill arm movement is mostly a pushing movement.

Side stepping can be taught at a fairly early stage in instructing beginners. It is a useful exercise to make pupils feel more comfortable on skis.

Vary instruction terrain as much as possible so that the pupils don't lock into a technique suitable only to a single incline. Start from the easy and go over to the more difficult and then back to the easy again. As proficiency increases, let pupils practice in loose and deep snow.

Stationary Turns

Stationary turns are not as important as they once were when equipment was far heavier, but they do have their place in instruction for beginners.

It's best to work stationary turn instruction into other instruction. For instance, when pupils are first learning the diagonal stride on parallel tracks, they can learn step turning to turn around at the end of their tracks. Kick turns and jump turns can also be taught in this manner.

Downhill Technique

The bulk of the world's ski-instruction literature seems to concentrate on the progression and methodology for teaching downhill running and downhill turns. Against this plethora background, it's necessary to make only a few observations specifically pertaining to downhill on touring and cross-country skis.

Instruct beginners and intermediate skiers on packed, but not hard, downhill slopes. Select a practice area with slopes of varying steepness.

Downhill running and turns with the flexible boot-binding-ski attachment of touring and cross-country gear requires a "feel" for terrain. Emphasize the use of terrain details to aid turns.

The basic downhill position is the wide-track stance with weight a bit on the heels for turns.

Keep the class moving; downhill practice is best combined with uphill skiing and vice versa.

Start with the simple and work up to the more difficult. A good turn progression starts with the snowplow turn, works through the stem turn and the stem christiania, and ends with the parallel and step-skating turns.

Good downhill technique is as important to cross-country racing as is good technique in any of the cross-country strides. Ever since the 1968 Winter Olympics in Autrans, France, where good downhill technique sometimes seemed the difference between a gold medal and fourth place, good downhill technique has been recognized as important for cross-country courses.

8

Racing Rules and Skiing Etiquette

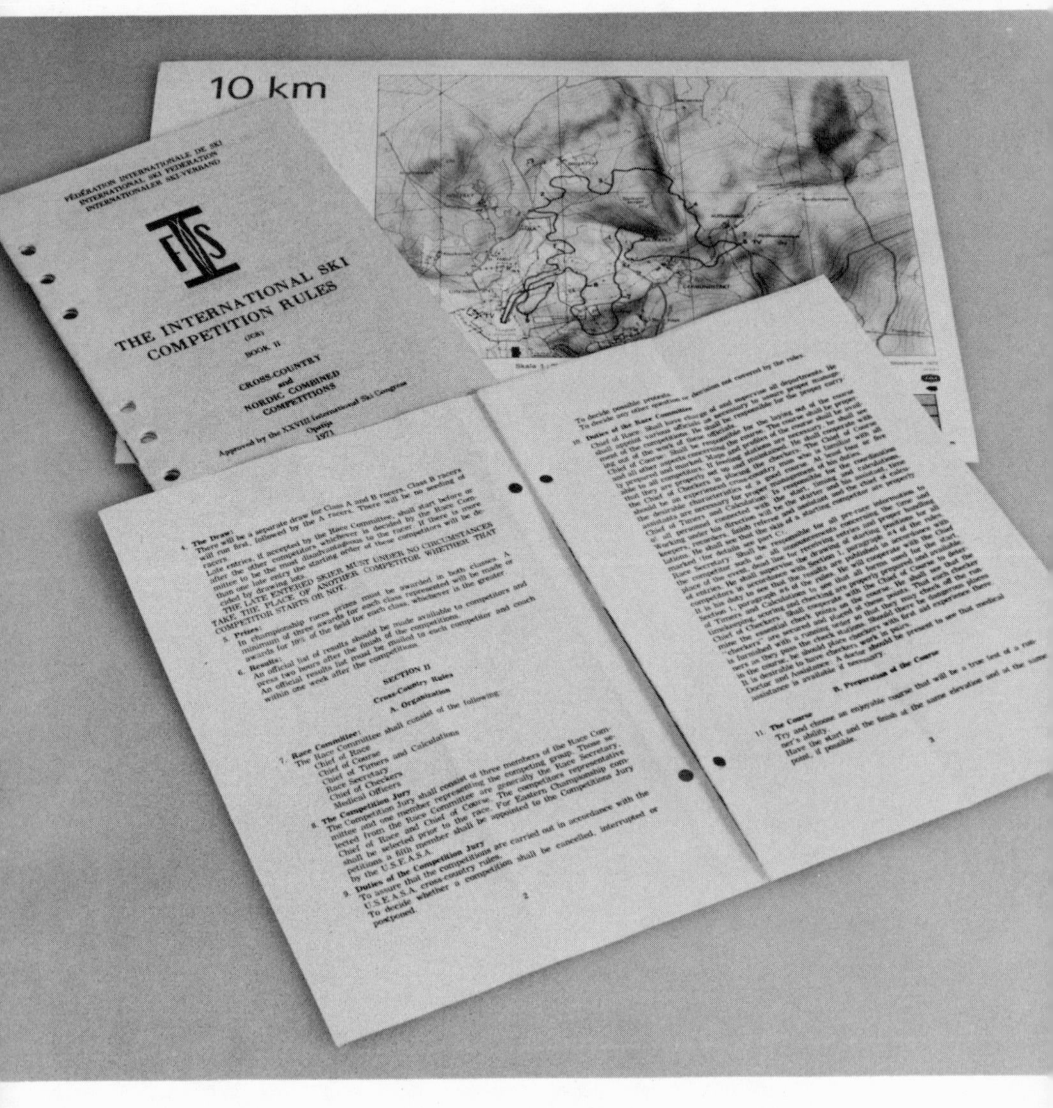
10 km
FÉDÉRATION INTERNATIONALE DE SKI
INTERNATIONAL SKI FEDERATION
INTERNATIONALER SKI-VERBAND
FIS
THE INTERNATIONAL SKI
COMPETITION RULES
(ICR)
BOOK II
CROSS-COUNTRY
and
NORDIC COMBINED
COMPETITIONS
Approved by the XXVIII International Ski Congress
Opatija
1971
SECTION II
Cross-Country Rules
A. Organization
B. Preparation of the Course

8

Racing Rules and Skiing Etiquette

RULES

The FIS (for *Fédération Internationale de Ski,* the international ski federation) rules govern all international ski competition, both Alpine and Nordic. The rules now governing cross-country are spelled out in a booklet entitled *The International Ski Competition Rules, Book II, Cross-Country and Nordic Combined Competitions* and have been in force since the 28th International Ski Congress in Opatija, Yugoslavia, in 1971.

Most of the forty-six member-countries of the FIS, including the United States, base their rules on the FIS rules. Decisions in disputes not specifically covered by national rules are usually referred to FIS rules. The FIS rules are available in English, French, and German, with the German text being basic and decisive.

Those portions of the FIS rules applying to racers, courses, and the conduct of races are summarized below. Departures of U.S. national rules from FIS rules are indicated. Both FIS and U.S. national rules are available from the United States Ski Association (USSA) in Denver.

Racers

The FIS defines juniors as girls eighteen years of age and younger and boys of nineteen and younger. Seniors are defined as women nineteen and older and men twenty and older. Age is defined as being that on December 31 of the previous calendar year; for instance, girls who are still eighteen and boys who are still nineteen as of December 31 can race as juniors the whole of the following year, regardless of the dates of their respective nineteenth and twentieth birthdays.

Juniors should normally start in their own classes. The Race Committee can make an exception allowing juniors to start with seniors when requested in writing by the racers' national association.

There are no age classes at FIS World Ski Championships or in the skiing event of the Winter Olympics.

In the United States, juniors are defined as all racers seventeen years of age and younger. Racers eighteen and older are divided into *A* and *B* classes. Any class *B* skier who has finished in the first five places in a major race during the previous season may be eligible for promotion to class *A*.

Events

There are five standard FIS course lengths, ranging from 5 kilometers (3.1 miles) up to 50 kilometers (31 miles). The course lengths raced depend on class: 10 and 15 kilometers for junior boys; 10, 15, 30, and 50 kilometers for men; 5 kilometers for junior girls; and 5 and 10 kilometers for women. U.S. men must be twenty years old or more to enter 30-km or longer races, which agrees with the FIS junior-senior definitions for these distances. All races longer than 50 km are classified as tour races and are not FIS events, although major tour races, such as Sweden's famed Vasaloppet, may be listed in national and FIS race calendars.

Individual events are those in which racers start individually at 30-second intervals. Pair starts are permitted for all but FIS World Ski Championship and Winter Olympic events. The individual men's 15-km race is called the 15-km special to differentiate it from the 15-km cross-country part of the Nordic combined.

Relays: Men's relays are 3 × 10 km or 4 × 10 km. Women's relays were 3 × 5 km until 1973; they are now 4 × 5 km. Members of a relay team in U.S. events must be members of the same club and must not have previously represented a different club during the current season.

Combined: The Nordic combined comprises 15-km cross-country ski racing and ski jumping on a hill having a norm point of 60 to 70 meters (for FIS World Ski Championships and Winter Olympics, the norm point must be 70 meters). U.S. rules stipulate the hill norm point as up to 40 meters for *C* competitions, and over 40 meters for *A* and *B* competitions.

Biathlon is a Nordic event combining cross-country skiing and shooting. It is a descendant of the older military patrol skiing event, which was included in the Winter Olympics prior to World War II but is now only a CISM event (for *Conseil International Militaire du Sport,* The International Military Sports Council). Biathlon is not a FIS event, but is under the jurisdiction of the UIPMB (*Union Internationale de Pentathlon Moderne et Biathlon,* The International Modern Pentathlon and Biathlon Association). Thus biathlon is a Winter Olympic, but not a FIS World Ski Championship event. There are two biathlon events: the individual, a Winter Olympic event since 1960, and the relay, a Winter Olympic event since 1968. The individual event comprises 4 shooting bouts on a 20-km cross-country course. The 4 × 7.5-km relay comprises 2 shooting bouts on each of its four laps. Courses are often laid out in loops using a single common range for all shooting.

In the United States, international biathlon is administered by a committee comprising members from the U.S. Modern Pentathlon and Biathlon Association, the USSA, the National Rifle Association (NRA), and the Army, Navy, Air Force, and Marine Corps. The U.S. training center is run by the Army in Alaska.

Types of U.S. Competition

There are two types of U.S. competition:

1 Major competitions in which competitors from more than three clubs compete, or which involve skiing organizations outside the jurisdiction of the USSA division involved.

2 Minor competitions of purely local interest which do not

Course	FIS Course Marking Color[a]	Maximum Height Difference (HD) in Meters
Junior		
girls, 5 km		100
boys, 10 km		150
boys, 15 km		200
Senior Women		
5 km	blue	100
relay, 4 × 5 km[b]	red/blue	100
10 km	violet	150
Senior Men		
special, 15 km	red	250
combined, 15 km	green	250
relay, 4 × 10 km	green/yellow	200
30 km	yellow	250
50 km	orange	250

[a]For individual events, start-number bib colors usually agre
is red, green, yellow, blue. U.S. courses may be marked w

[b]Prior to 1974, the FIS women's relay was 3 × 5 km.

involve more than three member clubs or organizations outside the USSA divisions involved.

Courses

In addition to its length, each course is described by three other numbers: the height difference *(HD)* between the highest and lowest points, the difference in height of any single climb *(MM)*, and total climbing or total elevation gained in the entire course *(MT)*.

At FIS World Ski Championships and Winter Olympics, the maximum permissible elevation of any part of a course is 1,650 meters (5,400 feet) above sea level. U.S. races, such as those in the Rocky Mountain States, must, of course, be run at higher elevations.

aximum Single Climb (MM) Meters	Total Climbing (MT)		
		Typical: 1974 FIS Courses, Falun, Sweden	
	Recommended in Meters	In Meters	In Feet
50	150–200		
75	250–400		
75	300–450		
50	150–200	170	556
50	150–200	160	525
75	250–300	330	1,082
100	450–600	525	1,722
100	400–500	450	1,476
100	300–450	360	1,182
100	750–1,000	990	3,250
100	1,000–1,500	1,480	4,860

h course marking colors. For relays, the sequence of bib colors
ed flags or streamers, with danger points marked with yellow.

LAYOUT A course should be laid out so as to be a technical, tactical, and physical test of the racers' capabilities. The course should be laid out as naturally as possible, varying the prescribed differences in height, climbs, flat, and downhill sections to avoid any monotony. In principle, courses should be ⅓ flat, ⅓ uphill, and ⅓ downhill. Where possible, a course should be laid out through woodland. The most strenuous climbs should not come in the first 2 or 3 kilometers, nor long downhills during the last kilometers. Rhythm should be broken as little as possible by too sudden or sharp changes of direction or by steep climbs, which force the racers to herringbone (or side-stepping for U.S. races). Downhills must be laid out so they can be skied without danger, even on a particularly fast or icy track. Changes of direction should occur before rather than at the end of downhill sections, and icy bends, sharp angles and narrow passages should be avoided.

A terrain profile and map of a course indicate its difficulty and compliance to these regulations.

At FIS World Ski Championships, courses or parts of courses may be run at most twice. As far as possible, the most difficult men's course should be the 15-km special, then the 10-km relay race, the 30 km, the 15-km Nordic combined, and the 50 km. For women, the corresponding ranking in terms of difficulty should be the 5 km, the 5-km relay, and the 10 km.

MEASUREMENT AND MARKING Measuring should be done by tape, marking each kilometer from the start with clearly visible boards. Courses should be marked in the direction of the race, using boards, arrows, flags and ribbons. Course marking must be so clear that the racers are never in doubt where the track goes. Signs should mark every completed 5 kilometers, and the last 5 kilometers of a race should be marked every kilometer. All changes of direction should be marked by clearly visible arrows. U.S. rules require mile or kilometer marking only for championship races.

The *start* and *finish* should normally be on the same level, side by side. For the relay, the start line is an arc of a circle of radius 100 meters. Parallel tracks spaced 2 meters apart should be provided, preferably one for each team starting. The last 500 meters (200 yards for U.S. races) before the finish and before the relay exchange must have a double track.

COURSE PREPARATION should begin long before snow falls, so that races can be run even with very little snow. Stones, tree trunks, roots, brush and similar obstacles should be removed, and narrow sections and turns should be widened. The course must be wide enough for double tracks and to permit the use of mechanical track-making devices if they are to be used in the winter. The U.S. rules stipulate 5 feet as the minimum width. Before a race, track preparation must be completed in time to allow for an official inspection. Tracks for skis and poles must be hard enough to permit full racing tempo, and downhills should permit full speed without danger. Mechanical track-making devices, such as track sleds drawn by snow scooters, are useful for rapid and

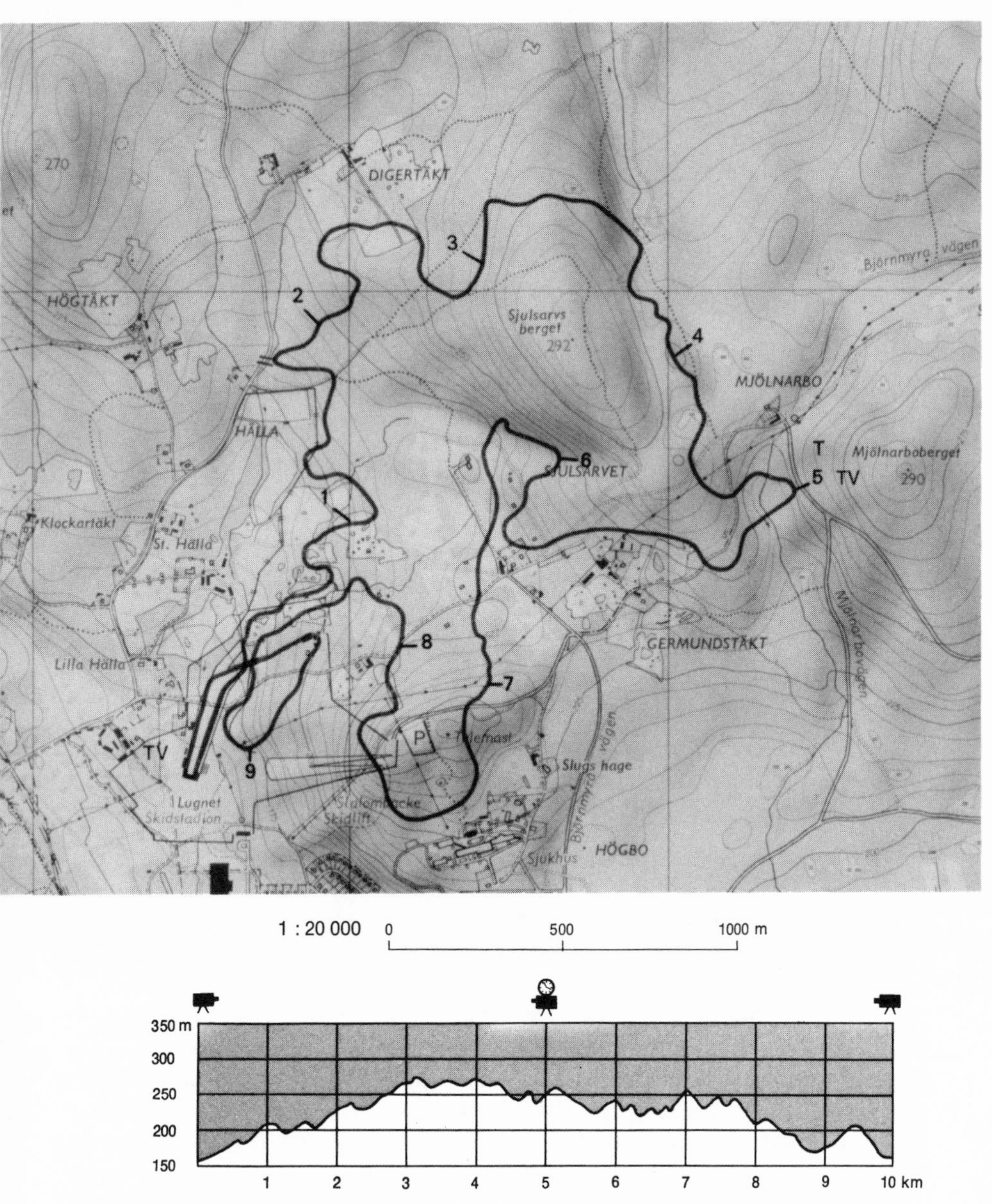

Typical course map and profile: 1974 FIS 10 km, Falun, Sweden

Track sleds can be drawn behind snow scooters for quick track setting.

efficient track preparation. Track sleds should set tracks spaced 4¾ to 7 inches between their inside edges on the flat, and 3¼ to 4¾ inches between their inside edges on uphills.

FEEDING, TEMPERATURE, AND INTERMEDIATE TIMING One feeding ("refreshment" in FIS terminology) station must be provided for courses up to 15 km, preferably located at the start and finish. Two stations are required for courses up to 30 km and four stations on courses up to 50 km; these stations must be placed so the racers can "feed" without loss of time or rhythm. Drinks such as warm sugar water, tea, fruit juices, etc., are most common at such stations. Wine, beer, or any other alcoholic beverages are forbidden. Snow and air temperatures should be taken at the start and finish area and at any other points of the course where extremes can be expected, such as high and low points, windy points, etc. One intermediate time should be taken for the 10-km race, for instance, at the 5-km point. Two should be taken for the 15-km and 30-km races, and at least three for the 50-km race.

Timing

Electric timing should be used whenever possible; it is obligatory for FIS World Ski Championships and Winter Olympic Games. Electric timing should always be checked with hand timing. Electric times are recorded to the nearest hundredth of a second, while hand times are recorded to the nearest tenth of a second. Timing for U.S. races may be to the nearest second.

Marking and Use of Skis and Poles

Both skis must be marked immediately before the start to prevent unauthorized change during the race. During the race, a racer may exchange both poles, but only one ski, without outside assistance. A racer may rewax during a race, but he must do so without assistance.

Health, Sex, and Doping

HEALTH The national ski associations are responsible for the health of the racers they enter in an international race.

SEX CONTROL A medical certificate of sex of all female racers is required for FIS World Ski Championship and Winter Olympic races. This certificate must be attached to the racer's entry and must not be more than four months old by the time of the start of the race in question. Compulsory medical examination should be avoided, but test examinations can be made.

DOPING CONTROL At all FIS World Ski Championship and Winter Olympic events, doping control is carried out following the sponsoring association's international rules.

SKIING ETIQUETTE

Touring skiers don't follow written rules as do cross-country racers, but there are a few "rules of the road" that make touring more enjoyable for all:

1 Courtesy is the law of the ski trail.

2 Keep to the right when meeting or being passed by another skier.

3 Yield the track to skiers coming downhill.

4 In touring, go out of the track to pass. Don't force your way past another skier if the trail is narrow.

5 Don't ski beyond your ability or faster than conditions permit on downhills. Give warning shouts on blind downhill turns and trail intersections.

6 If you stop, get out of the track.

7 Don't ski in or block race tracks.

8 Don't take a dog along on crowded ski tracks—it upsets the dog and can endanger other skiers.

9 Always aid an injured skier or otherwise help a skier in trouble.

10 Care for your surroundings. Don't be a litterbug—take your trash home.

9

Ski Touring and Tour Racing Worldwide

Eucalyptus trees and cross-country skiing can go together.

9

Ski Touring and Tour Racing Worldwide

Norwegians were responsible for introducing modern skiing to many countries. Even Alpine skiing, with its terminology such as "slalom," originated in Norway. But as time went on, starting in the 1930s and especially in the 1950s and 1960s, Central Europeans and North Americans came to dominate Alpine skiing. This dominance wasn't based only on the development of competitive skiing, but on the extensive development of recreational skiing involving enormous investments in hotels, lift facilities, and ski schools—all partially helped by top international race placings.

Thus Alpine skiing has become an important tourist industry in Central Europe and North America.

Until a few years ago, traditional ski touring and cross-country ski racing were virtually limited to the Nordic countries. In fact, cross-country ski racing was placed under the "Nordic disciplines" in international ski racing.

Thus, until recently, most people in Central Europe and North America thought exclusively of Alpine skiing at the mention of skis or skiing. Many still think this way today, even to the extent of calling Alpine skiing "regular skiing" and defining all other forms as something different from "regular." But the winds of change are blowing; touring skiers are growing in number, people are starting to find out that standing in a lift line is about as enjoyable as standing in a line in a bank or in a line for a subway. People are starting to find out that for beginners it's just as easy to ski downhill and turn on good touring gear as it is on Alpine gear. People are discovering that variation in skiing, going from one place to another, is more interesting than going up and down the same hill. And people are beginning to find out that ski touring is inherently far cheaper than Alpine skiing.

Tour ski races such as Sweden's famed Vasaloppet or Norway's tough trans-mountain Birkebeiner were pretty much limited to Swedes, Norwegians, and Finns ten years ago. Few outside Scandinavia seemed even to know of, much less appreciate, the idea of tour ski racing. But that's also changed. Names such as "Engadin" (Switzerland), "Marcialonga" (Italy), "Volkslanglauf" (Germany), "Washington's Birthday" (United States), and "Paddy Pallin" (Australia) are now well known even in Scandinavia.

The ski touring renaissance is most amazing in the United States, the country known worldwide as a nation of nonwalkers. Perhaps motivated by the upswing in interest in ecology or perhaps motivated by Kenneth Cooper's disturbing facts on the disadvantages of a sedentary life (in his *Aerobics* series of publications), Americans have taken to ski touring in a big way. In 1972, 350,000 pairs of touring and cross-country skis were sold in the United States (of which 185,000 pairs were imported from Norway).

The spread of ski touring in the United States is nothing less than an explosion. Ten years ago, there were no more than a couple of thousand touring skiers and cross-country racers in the entire country. Now there are more than half a million, and the total increases every season. Most large Alpine ski areas now have touring trails, and more and more tour races are organized every year.

The best example of the purely human value of ski touring is perhaps found in Canada. Particularly in western Canada, there are several minority groups such as Eskimos and Indians, and social friction exists, especially among children. Characteristic social problems such as higher-school dropout rates and juvenile delinquency were at one time prevalent. In 1963 the Northwest Territories recreation department invited fitness education expert Father J. M. Mouchet from Yukon in Alaska, to explore the potential human and physical resources related to outdoor fitness in the

Arctic. Father Mouchet recommended touring and cross-country skiing, chiefly because they were inexpensive and well suited to Northwest Canada's long ski season, from October 1 until the end of May. By 1967 Father Mouchet's skiing activities had grown beyond a simple community program. The Canadian National Fitness Council then approved a grant for a program to explore whether northern youth participating in an activity, if they have a chance of succeeding, could be motivated to greater achievement in life itself. The Territorial Experiment Ski Training (TEST) ski program was started at Lunvik, N.W.T., and Old Crow, Yukon. Over the following five years, the TEST program skiers did more than just well, entering and placing well against seasoned competition in major races including Olympics and FIS World Ski Championships. But most important, the program has focused more attention on Northwest Canada than could any amount of government propaganda, and the Indian and Eskimo youth have found that success on skis is more than just a hobby.

Italians have been cross-country racing internationally since the mid-1930s. By the 1960s, they had reached the winners' level. Their triumph was when Franco Nones won the 1968 Winter Olympic 30-km race in Autrans, France. Tour races were almost unknown in Italy until the late 1960s, but now major Italian tour races attract hundreds of starters, even for races of 70 km (44 miles).

Both West Germany and Switzerland have popularized ski touring on a nationwide basis through their state-sponsored ski federations as a part of physical-fitness programs. In West Germany, the *Volkslanglauf* ("People's Cross-Country") races have become the country's largest.

The East Germans have mustered an amazingly rapid assault on the citadel of international cross-country racing: in the 1974 FIS races, East Germans captured five of the twenty-one medals at stake in the cross-country events. Their basis for selecting racing talent is a broad spectrum of touring skiers and touring races for children.

The rolling mountains in Czechoslovakia are very much like those in Scandinavia. Today there are more than 2 million Czech touring skiers. The Czechs have organized their instruction of ski touring and have propagandized for the benefits of touring for many years. At the last INTERSKI (International Ski Instruction

Start of the 85.5 km (53 mile) Vasaloppet tour race, Sälen, Sweden

Congress) in Garmisch-Partenkirchen, the Czechs were responsible for the two major demonstrations of ski-touring instruction.

On the other side of the globe, Australia's Snowy Mountains in Victoria and New South Wales have become a ski-touring paradise. Skiing in Australia has primarily been Alpine and primarily been limited to the wealthy, chiefly because the snow and ski areas are so remote from population centers. But ski touring has now grown so much that more local groups can ski, and several high schools have made ski touring part of their physical education program. Annual tour races such as the Paddy Pallin Classic and the Charlie Derrick Memorial attract several hundred starters.

Russia has perhaps a healthy share of the world's best cross-country racers, chiefly because there are 6 million skiers in Russia, most of them touring skiers and cross-country racers. The Russians were cautious, not entering international cross-country races until the mid-1950s, but when they appeared, they took medals. Since they first entered international women's cross-country racing in 1954, Russians have dominated, taking a staggering twenty-one of the twenty-nine gold medals awarded through 1974. Russian men have often taken seemingly more than their share of medals and have numbered among the world's top skiers in the 1950s, 1960s, and 1970s. Russian cross-country coaches and officials maintain, as do their counterparts in many other countries, that good cross-country racing talent is available only through selection from a broad base of touring skiers *and* that a broad base of touring skiers is partially encouraged by top cross-country placings. This circle of events can well be responsible for the larger number of Russians who have become touring skiers over the past twenty years.

10

History in a Nutshell, Major Race Results

10

History in a Nutshell, Major Race Results

The following list summarizes the development in ski touring and cross-country ski racing since Norwegian miners first used skis in California in 1840. Ski history, which dates back some forty-five hundred years, is a subject in itself. For more complete works, see the literature list that follows this chapter.

YEAR	EVENT
1840	Norwegian miners ski in California
1850	Miners organize downhill ski races in California
1856	"Snowshoe" Thompson carries mail over mountains in California
1861	Trysil Ski and Gun Club, world's first, founded in Norway
1872	Nansen Ski Club, first in United States, founded in Berlin, N.Y.
1883	Foreningen til Ski-Idrettens Fremme (Society for the Furtherance of Ski Sports), world's first ski-competition organization, formed in Oslo

A historic cross-country photo from Finland. Handwritten text on back of original: "Old-fashioned skirt and modern knickers clothing for cross-country girls. No. 102 is Elsa Kumpulainen, twice Finnish champ; no. 132 is Miina Huttunan, four times Finnish champ. Picture taken in 1923."

1886	Aurora Ski Club founded in Red Wing, Minnesota, by 28 Norwegians
1887	Single pole replaced by two
1888	Fridtjof Nansen leads ski expedition across Greenland
1888	First 50-km cross-country ski race, Huseby meet (forerunner of Holmenkollen meet)
1890	First ski developed especially for cross-country ski racing

1890	First ski races in Colorado
1891	First laminated ski developed by H. M. Christiansen
1892	First Holmenkollen meet
1892	First toe binding developed by Svein Övergaard
1894	First toepiece developed by Fritz Huifeldt
1902	Skis first listed in U.S. catalog, Alex Taylor of New York: ladies' skis $5, gentlemen's skis $8
1903	First ski wax sold, Record tar wax made by Thomas Hansen
1904	First U.S. national ski meet, jumping in Ishpeming, Michigan
1908	Norwegian Ski Federation, world's first, founded
1910	Dartmouth College Ski Club, first U.S. collegiate skiing, founded
1910	First women's cross-country, Auran Club in Finland
1910	First international ski congress in Oslo, The International Ski Commission, founded
1914	Klister patented by Peter Östbye
1920	First 3-layer laminated ski
1922	First Vasaloppet from Sälen to Mora in Sweden, 85.6 km (54 miles) long
1924	The International Ski Commission disbanded, FIS founded
1924	Toe irons patented by Marius Eriksen

Auran Club, Lemi, Finland, cross-country team, circa 1910. This is the first known photo of women on a cross-country team.

1924	First Winter Olympics in Chamonix, France; Norwegian Thorleif Haug becomes world's first triple-gold-medal winner by winning 18 km and 50 km cross-country and Nordic combined, as well as taking bronze in jumping
1926	Rottefella binding patented by Bror With
1932	Winter Olympics in Lake Placid, N.Y., first time in United States
1933	Multilaminated skis patented by Splitkein

1933	First cross-country FIS relay, 4 × 10 km for men, Innsbruck, Austria
1942–45	U.S. Army Tenth Mountain Division established and trains in Colorado and Alaska, first U.S. ski troops
1948	First international cross-country for women, Sweden vs. Finland
1952	First women's cross-country in Winter Olympics, Oslo, 10 km
1954	First women's 10 km and 3 × 5 km relay in FIS, Falun, Sweden
1954	Men's 18-km race shortened to 15 km
1960	Winter Olympics in Squaw Valley, California, second time in United States
1962	Women cross-country skiers get three international events: 10 km, 5 km, and 3 × 5 km relay, in FIS, Zakopane, Poland; Alevtina Koltchina, USSR, wins three gold medals in cross-country
1968	John Bower wins Holmenkollen Nordic Combined King's Cup, first American to win major international Nordic meet
1970	First U.S. cross-country girls in FIS World Ski Championships, Vysoké Tatry, Czechoslovakia
1971–72	Ski-touring renaissance in United States: 350,000 pairs of touring skis (of which 277,000 pairs imported from Nordic countries) sold in 1972 vs. 170,000 pairs in 1971, twenty times as many as in 1966
1972	Colorado voters reject 1976 Denver Winter Olympics on state referendum; International Olympic Committee picks Innsbruck, Austria, as site for XIIth Olympic Winter Games

Russian Alevtina Koltjina, the first woman skier ever to win three World Ski Championship events: 1962 FIS 5 km, 10 km, and 3 × 5 km relay. Her feat was repeated by countrywomen racers Claudia Boyarskikh in the 1964 Winter Olympics and Galina Koulacova in the 1972 Winter Olympics and 1974 FIS Nordics. Photo taken at the 1966 FIS, in which Koltjina won two gold and one silver medal.

1972	Winter Olympics in Sapporo, Japan, first time in Asia
1973	Vasaloppet run for 50th time
1974	Women's 3 × 5 km relay replaced by 4 × 5 km relay. Russian Galina Kulakova becomes world's first skier to twice win all events, repeating her 1972 Winter Olympic performance in the FIS Nordic World Ski Championships, Falun, Sweden; first major race wins on fiberglass skis

Top: Norwegian Gjermund Eggen, the first cross-country man to win three World Ski Championship events: 1966 FIS 15 km, 50 km, and 4 × 10 km relay.

Bottom: King Olav V of Norway, himself once a noted Holmenkollen competitor, congratulating John Bower, USA, for winning the 1968 Holmenkollen combined King's Cup.

Top: Tim Caldwell, USA, just after placing second in the 1973 Holmenkollen 15-km race for juniors, then the best U.S. cross-country result to date. Teammate Bill Koch repeated Caldwell's performance, placing second in the 1974 Holmenkollen junior 15 km.

Bottom: U.S. cross-country women Allison Owen and Martha Rockwell in the 1974 FIS World Ski Championships 4 × 5 km relay, Falun, Sweden, the first four-lap event for U.S. women skiers.

THE BEST IN FIS WORLD SKI CHAMPIONSHIPS AND WINTER OLYMPICS

The International Ski Federation (FIS) is responsible for the skiing events of the Olympic Winter Games, held in leap years, and the FIS World Championships, held in even-numbered years between Olympic years. The FIS also arranged "Rendez-vous" races from 1925 to 1927, and "FIS-races" from 1928 to 1936.

The Olympic Winter Games are numbered consecutively with Roman numerals, starting with the first held in Chamonix in 1924. Following a 1965 FIS decision, all international races arranged by the FIS are regarded as world ski championships and are numbered consecutively starting with number one for the 1924 Olympic Winter Games.

The six best placings in the Olympic Winter Games (OWG), "Rendez-vous Race" (R-v-R), FIS race (FIS) and modern FIS World Ski Championships (no notation) are listed below. The international abbreviations for countries are:

AUT Austria	FIN Finland	SOV Russia
BRD W. Germany	FRA France	SUI Switzerland
BUL Bulgaria	ITA Italy	SWE Sweden
CAN Canada	GER Germany	USA United States
CSF Czechoslovakia	NOR Norway	
DDR E. Germany	POL Poland	

MEN'S CROSS-COUNTRY

No	Year	Country	Site	18 km	30 km	50 km
1	1924	FRA	Chamonix OWG I	1 Th. Haug NOR 2 J. Gröttumsbraaten NOR 3 T. Niku FIN 4 J. Maardalen NOR 5 E. Landvik NOR 6 P.-E. Hedlund SWE		1 Th. Haug NOR 2 Th. Strömstad NOR 3 J.Gröttumsbraaten NOR 4 J. Maardalen NOR 5 T. Persson SWE 6 E. Alm SWE
2	1925	CSF	Johannisbad R-v-R	1 O. Nemecky CSF 2 Fr. Donth CSF 3 J. Erleback CSF 4 J. Adolf CSF 5 J. Bräth CSF 6 G. Ghedina ITA		1 Fr. Donth CSF 2 Fr. Häckel CSF 3 A. Ettrich CSF 4 J. Adolf CSF 5 J. Erleback CSF 6 J. Nemecky CSF
3	1926	FIN	Lahti R-v-R		1 M. Raivio FIN 2 T. Lappalainen FIN 3 V. Saarinen FIN 4 G. Jonsson SWE 5 S. Åström SWE 6 M. Lappalainen FIN	1 M. Raivio FIN 2 T. Lappalainen FIN 3 O. Kjellbotn NOR 4 O. Hegge NOR 5 G. Jonsson SWE 6 T. Niku FIN
4	1927	ITA	Cortina d'Ampezzo R-v-R	1 J. Lindgren SWE 2 Fr. Donth CSF 3 V. Schneider GER 4 J. Wikström SWE 5 G. Müller GER 6 E. Huber GER		1 J. Lindgren SWE 2 J. Wikström SWE 3 Fr. Donth CSF 4 V. Demetz ITA 5 H. Theato GER 6 J. Nemecky CSF
5	1928	SUI	St. Moritz OWG II	1 J. Gröttumsbraaten NOR 2 O. Hegge NOR 3 R. Ödegaard NOR 4 V. Saarinen FIN 5 H. Haakonsen NOR 6 P.-E. Hedlund SWE		1 P.-E. Hedlund SWE 2 G. Jonsson SWE 3 V. Andersson SWE 4 O. Kjellbotn NOR 5 O. Hegge NOR 6 T. Lappalainen FIN
No	**Year**	**Country**	**Site**	**15–18 km**	**50 km**	**Relay, 4 × 10 km**
6	1929	POL	Zakopane	1 V. Saarinen FIN	1 A. Knuttila FIN	

				6 H. Haakonsen NOR	6 Hj. Bergström SWE	
7	1930	NOR	Oslo FIS	1 A. Rustadstuen NOR 2 T. Brodahl NOR 3 T. Lappalainen FIN 4 K. Hovde NOR 5 V. Saarinen FIN 6 M. Lappalainen FIN	1 S. Utterström SWE 2 A. Rustadstuen NOR 3 A. Paananen FIN 4 M. Lappalainen FIN 5 M.P. Vangli NOR 6 V. Saarinen FIN	
8	1931	GER	Oberhof FIS	1 J. Gröttumsbraaten NOR 2 Chr. Hovde NOR 3 N. Svärd SWE 4 K. Lindberg SWE 5 H. Vikzell SWE 6 P. Vangli NOR	1 O. Stenen NOR 2 P. Vangli NOR 3 K. Lindberg SWE 4 N. Svärd SWE 5 Chr. Hovde NOR 6 H. Vikzell SWE	
9	1932	USA	Lake Placid OWG III	1 S. Utterström SWE 2 A. Wikström SWE 3 V. Saarinen FIN 4 M. Lappalainen FIN 5 A. Rustadstuen NOR 6 J. Gröttumsbraaten NOR	1 V. Saarinen FIN 2 V. Liikanen FIN 3 A. Rustadstuen NOR 4 O. Hegge NOR 5 S. Vestad NOR 6 S. Utterström SWE	
10	1933	AUT	Innsbruck FIS	1 N. Englund SWE 2 Hj. Bergström SWE 3 V. Liikanen FIN 4 V. Saarinen FIN 5 S. Utterström SWE 6 F. Däuber GER	1 V. Saarinen FIN 2 S. Utterström SWE 3 Hj. Bergström SWE 4 V. Liikanen FIN 5 J.A. Persson SWE 6 P.-E. Hedlund SWE	1 SWE (P.-E. Hedlund, S. Utterström, N. Englund, Hj. Bergström) 2 CSF (Svaz) (F. Simunck, V. Novak, A. Barton, C. Musil) 3 AUT (H. Gstrein, H. Gadner, B. Niederkofler, H. Paumgarten) 4 GER (W. Motz, W. Bogner, J. Ponn, H. Leupold) 5 ITA (F. de Zulian, E. Vuerich, S. Seilligo, S. Menardi) 6 CSF (HDW) (F. Lauer, F. Kraus, A. Horn, F. Semptner)

11	1934	SWE	Sollefteå FIS	1 S. Nurmela 2 V. Saarinen 3 M. Lappalainen 4 A. Häggblad 5 K. Karppinen 6 O. Hagen	FIN FIN FIN SWE FIN NOR	1 E. Wiklund 2 N. Englund 3 O. Remes 4 A. Häggblad 5 J. Wikström 6 H. Wikström	SWE SWE FIN SWE SWE SWE	1 FIN (S. Nurmela, K. Karppinen, M. Lappalainen, V. Saarinen) 2 GER (W. Motz, J. Schweiner, W. Bogner, H. Leupold) 3 SWE (A. Karlsson, L. Th. Jonsson, N. Englund, A. Häggblad) 4 NOR (L. Bergendahl, O. Hoffsbakken, H. Vinjarengen, O. Hagen) 5 POL (B. Czech, S. Karpiel, S. Marusarz, A. Marusarz) 5 teams started
12	1935	CSF	Hohe Tatra FIS	1 K. Karppinen 2 O. Hagen 3 O. Hoffsbakken 4 S. Vestad 5 M. Matsbo 6 B. Iversen	FIN NOR NOR NOR SWE NOR	1 N. Englund 2 K. Karppinen 3 S. Brodahl 4 M. Husu 5 K. Ogi 6 M. Matsbo	SWE FIN NOR FIN SUI SWE	1 FIN (M. Husu, K. Karppinen, V. Liikunen, S. Nurmela) 2 NOR (S. Brodahl, B. Iversen, O. Hoffsbakken, O. Hagen) 3 SWE (H. Moritz, E. Larsson, M. Matsbo, N. Englund) 4 GER (M. Wörndle, H. Leupold, W. Motz, W. Bogner) 5 CSF (Svaz) (C. Musil, B. Kudery, F. Simunek, A. Barton) 6 CSF (HDW) (G. Berauer, F. Kraus, J. Ackermann, O. Berauer)
13	1936	GER	Garmisch-Parten-kirchen OWG IV	1 E. Larsson 2 O. Hagen 3 P. Niemi 4 M. Matsbo 5 O. Hoffsbakken 6 A. Rustadstuen	SWE NOR FIN SWE NOR NOR	1 E. Wiklund 2 A. Wikström 3 N. Englund 4 H. Bergström 5 K. Karppinen 6 A. Tuft	SWE SWE SWE SWE FIN NOR	1 FIN (S. Nurmela, K. Karppinen, M. Lähde, K. Jalkanen) 2 NOR (O. Hagen, O. Hoffsbakken, S. Brodahl, B. Iversen) 3 SWE (J. Berger, E.

						Kasebacher) 5 CSF (C.Musil, G.Berauer, L.Mihalak, F.Simonek) 6 GER (F. Däuber, W. Bogner, H. Leupold, T. Zellev)
14	1937	FRA	Chamonix	1 L. Bergendahl NOR 2 K. Jalkanen FIN 3 P. Niemi FIN 4 S. Hansson SWE 5 J. Kurikkala FIN 6 A. Dahlqvist SWE	1 P. Niemi FIN 2 K. Karppinen FIN 3 V. Demetz ITA 4 K. Jalkanen FIN 5 L. Bergendahl NOR 6 F. Smoleij JUG	1 NOR (A. Ryen, O. Fredriksen, S. Röen, L. Bergendahl) 2 FIN (P. Niemi, K. Karppinen, J. Kurikkala, K. Jalkanen) 3 ITA (G. Gerardi, A. Compagnoni, S. Confortola, V. Demetz) 4 SWE (S. Hansson, B. Stridsman, A. Hägglund, A. Dahlqvist) 5 CSF (C. Musil, G. Berauer, R. Vrana, F. Simonek) 6 SUI (A. Freiburghaus, J. Sonderegger, E. Berger, A. Limascher)
15	1938	FIN	Lahti	1 P. Pitkänen FIN 2 A. Dahlqvist SWE 3 K. Jalkanen FIN 4 M. Matsbo SWE 5 M. Lauronen FIN 6 J. Kurikkala FIN	1 K. Jalkanen FIN 2 A. Rantalahti FIN 3 L. Bergendahl NOR 4 P. Niemi FIN 5 K. Karppinen FIN 6 T. Tiainen FIN	1 FIN (J. Kurikkala, M. Lauronen, P. Pitkänen, K. Karppinen) 2 NOR (R. Ringstad, O. Ökern, A.Larsen, L. Bergendahl) 3 SWE (S. Hansson, D. Johansson, S. Nilsson, M. Matsbo) 4 SUI (A. Freiburghaus, A. Gamma, E. Anderegg, E. Soguel) 5 GER (E. Haberle, G. Merlz, W. Bogner, H. Leupold) 6 ITA (G. Gerardi, G. Bauer, A. Jammeron, V. Demetz)

No	Year	Country	Site	18 km	30 km	50 km	Relay, 4 × 10 km
16	1939	POL	Zakopane	1 J. Kurikkala FIN 2 K. Karppinen FIN 3 C. Pahlin SWE 4 K. Jalkanen FIN 5 L. Bergendahl NOR 6 P. Niemi FIN		1 L. Bergendahl NOR 2 K. Karppinen FIN 3 O. Gjöslien NOR 4 P. Vanninen FIN 5 P. Niemi FIN 6 A. Hägglund SWE	1 FIN (P. Pitkänen, O. Alakulppi, E. Olkinuora, K. Karppinen) 2 SWE (A. Hägglund, S. Stenvall, J. Westbergh, C. Pahlin) 3 ITA (A. Compagnoni, S. Compagnoni, G. Bauer, A. Jammeron) 4 NOR (O. Odden, M. Fosseide, E. Evensen, O. Hoffsbakken) 5 SUI (A. Freiburghaus, E. Soguel, V. Borghi, A. Gamma) 6 GER (G. Lochbihler, R. Wöss, L. Bach, A. Burk)
17	1948	SUI	St.Moritz OWG V	1 M. Lundström SWE 2 N. Östensson SWE 3 G. Eriksson SWE 4 H. Hasu FIN 5 N. Karlsson SWE 6 S. Rytky FIN		1 N. Karlsson SWE 2 H. Eriksson SWE 3 B. Vanninen FIN 4 P. Vanninen FIN 5 A.Törnkvist SWE 6 E. Schild SUI	1 SWE (N. Östensson, N. Täpp, G. Eriksson, M. Lundström) 2 FIN (L. Silvennoinen, T. Laukkanen, S. Rytky, A. Kiuru) 3 NOR (E. Evensen, O. Ökern, R. Nyborg, O. Hagen) 4 AUT (J. Gstrein, J. Deutschmann, E. Hundertpfund, C. Rafreider) 5 SUI (N. Stump, R. Zurbriggen, M. Müller, E. Schild) 6 ITA (V. Perruchon, S. Confortola, R. Rodighiero, S. Compagnoni)
18	1950	USA	Lake Placid Rumford	1 K.-E. Åström SWE 2 E. Josefsson SWE 3 A. Nyaas NOR 4 A. Kiuru FIN 5 P. Lonkila FIN 6 V. Vellonen FIN		1 G. Eriksson SWE 2 E. Josefsson SWE 3 N. Karlsson SWE 4 A. Törnkvist SWE 5 H. Maartmann NOR 6 P. Vanninen FIN	1 SWE (N. Täpp, K.-E. Åström, M. Lundström, E. Josefsson) 2 FIN (H. Hasu, V. Vellonen, P. Lonkila, A. Kiuru)

							Carrara) 5 USA (S. Dunklee, R. Townsend, L. Hawkenson, D. Johnson) 6 CAN (C. Richer, I. Wahlberg, A. Alain, T. Dennie)
19	1952	NOR	Oslo OWG VI	1 H. Brenden NOR 2 T. Mäkelä FIN 3 P. Lonkila FIN 4 H. Hasu FIN 5 N. Karlsson SWE 6 M. Stokken NOR		1 V. Hakulinen FIN 2 E. Kolehmainen FIN 3 M. Estenstad NOR 4 O. Ökern NOR 5 K. Mononen FIN 6 N. Karlsson SWE	1 FIN (H. Hasu, P. Lonkila, U. Korhonen, T. Mäkelä) 2 NOR (M. Estenstad, M. Kirkholt, M. Stokken, H. Brenden) 3 SWE (N. Täpp, S. Andersson, E. Josefsson, M. Lundström) 4 FRA (G. Perrier, B. Carrara, J. Mermet, R. Mandrillon) 5 AUT (H. Eder, F. Krischan, C. Rafreider, J. Schneeberger) 6 ITA (A. Delladio, N. Anderlini, F. deFlorian, V. Perruchon)
20	1954	SWE	Falun	**15 km** 1 V. Hakulinen FIN 2 A. Viitanen FIN 3 A. Kiuru FIN 4 F. Terentjev SOV 5 T. Mäkelä FIN 6 V. Räsänen FIN	1 V. Kusin SOV 2 V. Hakulinen FIN 3 M. Lautala FIN 4 S. Jernberg SWE 5 T. Sipilä FIN 6 E. Tilli FIN	1 V. Kusin SOV 2 V. Hakulinen FIN 3 A. Viitanen FIN 4 M. Stokken NOR 5 E. Landsem NOR 6 F. Terentjev SOV	1 FIN (A. Kiuru, T. Mäkelä, A. Viitanen, V. Hakulinen) 2 SOV (N. Koslov, F. Terentjev, A. Kusnetsov, V. Kusin) 3 SWE (S. Larsson, S. Jernberg, A. Olsson, P.-E. Larsson) 4 NOR (H. Brusveen, O. Lykkja, M. Stokken, H. Brenden) 5 ITA (V. Cchiocchetti, A. Delladio, F. deFlorian, O. Compagnoni) 6 FRA (R. Mandrillon, S. Mercier, J. Mermet, B. Carrara)

21	1956	ITA	Cortina d'Ampezzo OWG VII	1 H. Brenden NOR 2 S. Jernberg SWE 3 P. Kolchin SOV 4 V. Hakulinen FIN 5 H. Brusveen NOR 6 M. Stokken NOR	1 V. Hakulinen FIN 2 S. Jernberg SWE 3 P. Kolchin SOV 4 A. Sheljukhin SOV 5 V. Kusin SOV 6 F. Terentjev SOV	1 S. Jernberg SWE 2 V. Hakulinen FIN 3 F. Terentjev SOV 4 E. Kolehmainen FIN 5 A. Sheljukhin SOV 6 P. Kolchin SOV	1 SOV (F. Terentjev, P. Kolchin, N. Anikin, V. Kusin) 2 FIN (A. Kiuru, J. Kortelainen, A. Viitanen, V. Hakulinen) 3 SWE (L. Larsson, G.Samuelsson, P.-E. Larsson, S.Jernberg) 4 NOR (H. Brusveen, P. Olsen, M. Stokken, H. Brenden) 5 ITA (P. Fattor, O. Compagnoni, I. Chatrian, F. deFlorian) 6 FRA (V. Arbez, R. Mandrillon, B. Carrara, J. Mermet)
22	1958	FIN	Lahti	1 V. Hakulinen FIN 2 P. Koltjin SOV 3 A. Sheljukhin SOV 4 S. Jernberg SWE 5 H. Brusveen NOR 6 F. Terentjev SOV	1 K. Hämäläinen FIN 2 P. Koltjin SOV 3 S. Jernberg SWE 4 A. Viitanen FIN 5 A. Tiainen FIN 6 V. Hakulinen FIN	1 S. Jernberg SWE 2 V. Hakulinen FIN 3 A. Viitanen FIN 4 A. Tiainen FIN 5 E. Kolehmainen FIN 6 P. Koltjin SOV	1 SWE (S. Jernberg, L. Larsson, S. Grahn, P.-E. Larsson) 2 SOV (F. Terentjev, N. Anikin, A. Sheljukhin, P. Koltjin) 3 FIN (K. Hämäläinen, A. Tiainen, A. Viitanen, V. Hakulinen) 4 NOR (H. Brenden, O. Jensen, M. Stokken, H. Brusveen) 5 ITA (F. deFlorian, O. Compagnoni, M. deFlorian, G. Steiner) 6 FRA (V. Arbez, R. Mandrillon, B. Carrara, J. Mermet)
23	1960	USA	Squaw Valley OWG VIII	1 H. Brusveen NOR 2 S. Jernberg SWE 3 V. Hakulinen FIN 4 G. Vaganov SOV	1 S. Jernberg SWE 2 R. Rämgård SWE 3 N. Anikin SOV 4 G. Vaganov SOV	1 K. Hämäläinen FIN 2 V. Hakulinen FIN 3 R. Rämgård SWE 4 L. Larsson SWE	1 FIN (T. Alatalo, E. Mäntyranta, V. Huhtala, V. Hakulinen) 2 NOR (H. Grönningen, H.

	Year	Country	Site	15 km	30 km	50 km	Relay, 4 × 10 km
							Anikin) 4 SWE (L. Olsson, J. Stefansson, L. Larsson, S. Jernberg) 5 ITA (G. deFlorian, G. Steiner, P. Fattor. M. deDorigo) 6 POL (A. Meteja, J. Rysula, J. Gut-Misiaga, K. Zelek)
24	1962	POL	Zakopane	1 A. Rönnlund SWE 2 H. Grönningen NOR 3 E. Östby NOR 4 M. Lundemo NOR 5 E. Mäntyranta FIN 6 J. Stefansson SWE	1 E. Mäntyranta FIN 2 J. Stefansson SWE 3 G. de Florian ITA 4 H. Grönningen NOR 5 E. Östby NOR 6 A. Rönnlund SWE	1 S. Jernberg SWE 2 A. Rönnlund SWE 3 K. Hämäläinen FIN 4 A. Tiainen FIN 5 H. Grönningen NOR 6 J. Stefansson SWE	1 SWE (L. Olsson, S. Grahn, S. Jernberg, A. Rönnlund) 2 FIN (V. Huhtala, K. Laurila, P. Pesonen, E. Mäntyranta) 3 SOV (J. Utrobin, P. Koltjin, A. Kuznetsov, G. Vaganov) 4 NOR (M. Lundemo, H. Brenden, E. ⅝stby, H. Grönningen) 5 ITA (G. Steiner, G. Stella, M. de Dorigo, G. de Florian) 6 FRA (F. Mathieu, R. Secretant, V. Arbez, J. Mermet)
25	1964	AUT	Innsbruck OWG IX	1 E. Mäntyranta FIN 2 H. Grönningen NOR 3 S. Jernberg SWE 4 V. Huhtala FIN 5 J. Stefansson SWE 6 P. Koltjin SOV	1 E. Mäntyranta FIN 2 H. Grönningen NOR 3 I. Voronchikhin SOV 4 J. Stefansson SWE 5 S. Jernberg SWE 6 K. Laurila FIN	1 S. Jernberg SWE 2 A. Rönnlund SWE 3 A. Tiainen FIN 4 J. Stefansson SWE 5 S. Stensheim NOR 6 H. Grönningen NOR	1 SWE (K.-A. Asph, S. Jernberg, J. Stefansson, A. Rönnlund) 2 FIN (V. Huhtala, A. Tiainen, K. Laurila, E. Mäntyranta) 3 SOV (I. Utrobin, G. Vaganov, I. Voronchikhin, P. Koltjin) 4 NOR (M. Lundemo, E. Steineide, E. Östby, H. Grönningen) 5 ITA (G. Steiner, M. de Dorigo, G. de Florian, F. Nones) 6 FRA (V. Arbez, F. Mathieu, R. Pires, P. Romand)

26	1966	NOR	Oslo	1 Gj. Eggen NOR 2 O. Ellefsaeter NOR 3 O. Martinsen NOR 4 Bj. Andersson SWE 5 K. Laurila FIN 6 E. Mäntyranta FIN	1 E. Mäntyranta FIN 2 K. Laurila FIN 3 W. Demel BRD 4 I. Sandström SWE 5 A. Akentjev SOV 6 F. Nones ITA	1 Gj. Eggen NOR 2 A. Tiainen FIN 3 E. Mäntyranta FIN 4 O. Ellefsaeter NOR 5 H. Taipale FIN 6 V. Vedenin SOV	1 NOR (O. Martinsen, H. Grönningen, O. Ellesfsaeter, Gj. Eggen) 2 FIN (K. Oikarainen, H. Taipale, K. Laurila, E. Mäntyranta) 3 ITA (G. de Florian, F. Nones, G. Stella, F. Manfroi) 4 SWE (Kj. Lidh, Bj. Andersson, K.-Å. Asph, I. Sandström) 5 SOV (I. Utrobin, V. Vedenin, A. Nasedkin, A. Akentjev) 6 SUI (K. Hischier, J. Haas, D. Mast, A. Kaelin)
27	1968	FRA	Grenoble OWG X	1 H. Grönningen NOR 2 E. Mäntyranta FIN 3 G. Larsson SWE 4 K. Laurila FIN 5 J. Halvarsson SWE 6 Bj. Andersson SWE	1 F. Nones ITA 2 O. Martinsen NOR 3 E. Mäntyranta FIN 4 V. Voronkov SOV 5 G. de Florian ITA 6 K. Laurila FIN	1 O. Ellefsaeter NOR 2 V. Vedenin SOV 3 J. Haas SUI 4 P. Tyldum NOR 5 M. Risberg SWE 6 G. Larsson SWE	1 NOR (O. Martinsen, P. Tyldum, H. Gränningen, O. Ellefsaeter) 2 SWE (J. Halvarsson, Bj. Andersson, G. Larsson, A. Rönnlund) 3 FIN (K. Oikarainen, H. Taipale, K. Laurila, E. Mäntyranta) 4 SOV (V. Voronkov, A. Akentjev, V. Tarakanov, V. Vedenin) 5 SUI (K. Hischier, J. Haas, F. Koch, A. Kaelin) 6 ITA (G. de Florian, F. Nones, P. Serafini, A. Stella)
28	1970	CSF	Vysoké Tatry	1 L. G. Åslund SWE 2 O. Martinsen NOR 3 F. Simasov SOV 4 G. D. Klause DDR 5 P. Tyldum NOR 6 V. Tarakanov SOV	1 V. Vedenin SOV 2 G. Grimmer DDR 3 O. Martinsen NOR 4 P. Tyldum NOR 5 G. D. Klause DDR 6 L. G. Åslund SWE	1 K. Oikarainen FIN 2 V. Vedenin SOV 3 G. Grimmer DDR 4 F. Simasov SOV 5 L. G. Åslund SWE 6 W. Demel BRD	1 SOV (V. Voronkov, V. Tarakanov, F. Simasov, V. Vedenin) 2 DDR (G. Hessler, A. Lesser, G. Grimmer, G. D. Klause) 3 SWE (O. Lestander, J. Halvarsson, I. Sandström, L. G. Åslund) 4 NOR (O. Martinsen, H.

							6 ITA (F. Nones, R. Primus, G. Stella, U. Kostner)
29	1972	JPN	Sapporo OWG XI	1 S.-A. Lundbäck SWE 2 F. Simaschov SOV 3 I. Formo NOR 4 J. Mieto FIN 5 Y. Skobov SOV 6 A. Lesser DDR	1 V. Vedenin SOV 2 P. Tyldum NOR 3 J. Harviken NOR 4 G. Larsson SWE 5 W. Demel BRD 6 F. Simaschov SOV	1 P. Tyldum NOR 2 M. Myrmo NOR 3 V. Vedenin SOV 4 R. Hjermstad NOR 5 W. Demel BRD 6 W. Geeser SUI	1 SOV (V. Voronkov, Y. Skobov, F. Simaschov, V. Vedenin) 2 NOR (O. Braa, P. Tyldum, I. Formo, J. Harviken) 3 SUI (A. Kälin, A. Giger, A. Kälin, E. Hauser) 4 SWE (T. Magnusson, L.-G. Åslund, G. Larsson, S.-Å. Lundbäck) 5 FIN (H. Taipale, J. Mieto, J. Repo, O. Karjalainen) 6 DDR (G. Hessler, A. Lesser, G. Grimmer, G.-D. Klause)
30	1974	SWE	Falun	1 M. Myrmo NOR 2 G. Grimmer DDR 3 V. Rochev SOV 4 J. Mieto FIN 5 O. Braa NOR 6 I. Formo NOR	1 T. Magnusson SWE 2 J. Meito FIN 3 J. Staszel POL 4 I. Garanin SOV 5 L.-G. Aslund SWE 6 G. Grimmer DDR	1 G. Grimmer DDR 2 S. Henych CSF 3 T. Magnusson SWE 4 S-Å Lundbäck SWE 5 V. Rochev SOV 6 A. Biriukov SOV	1 DDR (G. Hessler, D. Meinel, G. Grimmer, G.-D. Klause) 2 SOV (I. Garanin, F. Simashev, V. Rochev, Y. Skobov) 3 NOR (M. Myrmo, O. Martinsen, I. Formo, O. Braa) 4 FIN (R. Lehtinen, K. Laurile, O. Karjalainen, J. Mieto) 5 CSF (F. Simon, J. Beran, J. Fajstavr, S. Henych) 6 SUI (A. Kälin, A. Giger, E. Hauser, W. Geeser)

WOMEN'S CROSS-COUNTRY

No	Year	Country	Site	5 km	10 km	Relay, 3 × 5 km
19	1952	NOR	Oslo OWG VI		1 L. Wideman FIN 2 M. Hietamies FIN 3 S. Rantanen FIN 4 M. Norberg SWE 5 S. Polkunen FIN 6 R. Wahl NOR	
20	1954	SWE	Falun		1 L. Kozyreva SOV 2 S. Rantanen FIN 3 M. Hietamies FIN 4 M. Maslennikova SOV 5 A. Leontjeva SOV 6 S. Polkunen FIN	1 SOV (L. Kozyreva, M. Maslennikova, V. Tsareva) 2 FIN (S. Polkunen, M. Hietamies, S. Rantanen) 3 SWE (A.-L. Eriksson, M. Norberg, S. Edström) 4 NOR (K. Gutubakken, M. Öiseth, R. Wahl) 5 CSF (O. Krasilová, M. Bartaková, E. Vasiková) 6 ITA (E. Mus, A. Parmesani, I. Taffra)
21	1956	ITA	Cortina d'Ampezzo OWG VII		1 L. Kozyreva SOV 2 R. Eroshina SOV 3 S. Edström SWE 4 A. Koltjina SOV 5 S. Rantanen FIN 6 M. Hietamies FIN	1 FIN (S. Polkunen, M. Hietamies, S. Rantanen) 2 SOV (L. Kozyreva, A. Koltjina, R. Eroshina) 3 SWE (I. Johansson, A.-L. Eriksson, S. Edström) 4 NOR (K. Brusveen, G. Regland, R. Wahl) 5 POL (M. Bukova-Gasienica, J. Peksa, Z. Krzeptowska) 6 CSF (E. Benesova, L. Patockova, E. Lauermannova)
22	1958	FIN	Lahti		1 A. Koltjina SOV 2 L. Kozyreva SOV 3 S. Rantanen FIN 4 R. Eroshina SOV 5 E. Smirnova SOV 6 M. Gusakova SOV	1 SOV (R. Eroshina, A. Koltjina, L. Kozyreva) 2 FIN (T. Mikkula-Pöysti, P. Korkee, S. Rantanen) 3 SWE (M. Norberg, I. Johansson, S. Edström) 4 POL (M.

						6 DDR (Chr. Göhler, E. Spiegelhauer, S. Kallus)
23	1960	USA	Squaw Valley OWG VIII		1 M. Gusakova SOV 2 L. Baranova-Kozyreva SOV 3 R. Eroshina SOV 4 A. Koltjina SOV 5 S. Edström-Ruthström SWE 6 T. Pöysti FIN	1 SWE (I. Johansson, B. Strandberg, S. Edström-Ruthström) 2 SOV (R. Eroshina, M. Gusakova, L. Baranova-Kozyreva) 3 FIN (S. Rantanen, E. Ruoppa, T. Pöysti) 4 POL (S. Biegun, H. Gasieniac-Daniel, J. Peksa-Czerniawska) 5 DDR (R. Czech-Blasl, R, Borges, S. Kallus-Hausschild)
24	1962	POL	Zakopane	1 A. Koltjina SOV 2 L. Baranova SOV 3 M. Gusakova SOV 4 S. Rantanen FIN 5 M. Lehtonen FIN 6 E. Mekshilo SOV	1 A. Koltjina SOV 2 M. Gusakova SOV 3 R. Eroshina SOV 4 L. Baranova SOV 5 M. Lehtonen FIN 6 B. Martinsson SWE	1 SOV (L. Baranova, M. Gusakova, A. Koltjina) 2 SWE (B. Martinsson, B. Strandberg, T. Gustafsson) 3 FIN (S. Rantanen, R. Ruoppa, M. Lehtenen) 4 POL (W. Stempak, J. Czerniawska, S. Biegun) 5 DDR (R. Dannhauer, Chr. Herklotz, S. Kallus) 6 CSF (V. Srnkova, J. Skodova, E. Paulusova)
25	1964	AUT	Innsbruck OWG IX	1 C. Boyarskikh SOV 2 M. Lehtonen FIN 3 A. Koltjina SOV 4 E. Mekshilo SOV 5 T. Pöysti FIN 6 T. Gustafsson SWE	1 C. Boyarskikh SOV 2 E. Mekshilo SOV 3 M. Gusakova SOV 4 B. Strandberg SWE 5 T. Pöysti FIN 6 S. Pusula FIN	1 SOV (A. Koltjina, E. Mekshilo, C. Boyarskikh) 2 SWE (B. Martinsson, B. Strandberg, T. Gustafsson) 3 FIN (S. Pusula, T. Pöysti, M. Lehtonen) 4 DDR (C. Nestler, R. Czech-Blasl, R. Dannhauer) 5 BUL (R. Dimova, N. Vassileva, K. Stoeva) 6 CSF (J. Skodova, E. Brizova, E. Paulusova)

26	1966	NOR	Oslo	1 A. Koltjina SOV 2 C. Boyarskikh SOV 3 R. Achkina SOV 4 E. Mekshilo SOV 5 K. Stoeva BUL 6 T. Gustafsson SWE	1 C. Boyarskikh SOV 2 A. Koltjina SOV 3 T. Gustafsson SWE 4 E. Mekshilo SOV 5 K. Stoeva BUL 6 B. Martinsson SWE	1 SOV (C. Boyarskikh, R. Achkina, A. Koltjina) 2 NOR (I. Wigernaes, I. Aufles, B. Mördre) 3 SWE (B. Martinsson, B. Strandberg, T. Gustafsson) 4 DDR (G. Nobis, A. Unger, Chr. Nestler) 5 FIN (T. Pöysti, E. Ruoppa, S. Pusula) 6 BUL (K. Stoeva, N. Vassileva, V. Pandeva)
27	1968	FRA	Grenoble OWG X	1 Toini Gustafsson SWE 2 Galina Kulakova SOV 3 Alevtina Koltjina SOV 4 Barbro Martinsson SWE 5 Marjatta Kajosmaa FIN 6 Rita Achkina SOV	1 Toini Gustafsson SWE 2 Berit Mördre NOR 3 Inger Aufles NOR 4 Barbro Martinsson SWE 5 Marjatta Kajosmaa FIN 6 Galina Kulakova SOV	1 NOR (I. Aufles, B. Enger-Damon, B. Mördre) 2 SWE (B. Strandberg, T. Gustafsson, B. Martinsson) 3 SOV (A. Koltjina, R. Achkina, G. Kulakova) 4 FIN (S. Pusula, M. Olkkonen, M. Kajosmaa) 5 POL (W. Budny, J. Czerniawska, S. Biegun) 6 DDR (R. Kohler, G. Schmid, Chr. Nestler)
28	1970	CSF	Vysoké Tatry	1 G. Kulakova SOV 2 G. Piljusenko SOV 3 N. Fjodorova SOV 4 M. Kajosmaa FIN 5 M. Endler BRD 6 S. Pusula FIN	1 A. Oljunina SOV 2 M. Kajosmaa FIN 3 G. Kulakova SOV 4 H. Sikolova CSF 5 R. Fischer DDR 6 G. Piljusenko SOV	1 SOV (N. Fjodorova, G. Kulakova, A. Oljunina) 2 DDR (G. Haupt, R. Fischer, A. Unger) 3 FIN (S. Pusula, H. Takalo, M. Kajosmaa) 4 NOR (I. Aufles, A. Dahl, B. Mördre-Lammedal) 5 CSF (M. Cillerova, H. Sikolova, M. Chlumova) 6 BRD (M. Mrklas, I.

No	Year	Country	Site	5 km		10 km		Relay, 4 × 5 km
			OWG XI	2 M. Kajosmaa 3 H. Sikolova 4 A. Oljunina 5 H. Kuntola 6 L. Moukhatcheva	FIN CSF SOV FIN SOV	2 A. Oljunina 3 M. Kajosmaa 4 L. Moukhatcheva 5 H. Takalo 6 A. Dahl	SOV FIN SOV FIN NOR	Oljunina, G. Kulakova) 2 FIN (H. Takalo, H. Kuntola, M. Kajosmaa) 3 NOR (I. Aufles, A. Dahl, B. Mörde-Lammedal) 4 BRD (M. Mrklas, I. Roth-Fuss, M. Endler) 5 DDR (G. Haupt, R. Fischer, A. Unger) 6 CSF (A. Bartosova, H. Sikolova, M. Cillerova)

No	Year	Country	Site	5 km		10 km		Relay, 4 × 5 km
30	1974	SWE	Falun	1 G. Kulakova 2 B. Paulü 3 R. Smetanina 4 B. Petzold 5 N. Baldycheva 6 U. Fossen	SOV CSF SOV DDR SOV NOR	1 G. Kulakova 2 B. Petzold 3 H. Takalo 4 B. Paulü 5 V. Schmidt 6 B. M.-Lammedal	SOV DDR FIN CSF DDR NOR	1 SOV (N. Baldicheva, N. Seljunina, R. Smetanina, G. Kulakova) 2 DDR (S. Krause, P. Hinze, P. Petzold, V. Schmidt) 3 CSF (A. Bartosova, G. Sekajova, M. Jaskovska, B. Paulü) 4 FIN (L. Suihkonen, H. Takalo, M. Kajosmaa, H. Kuntola) 5 SWE (L. Carlzon, G. Partapuoli, G. Fröjd, M. Bodelid) 6 NOR (U. Fossen, K. Mo-Berge, A. Dahl, B.

Selected Literature

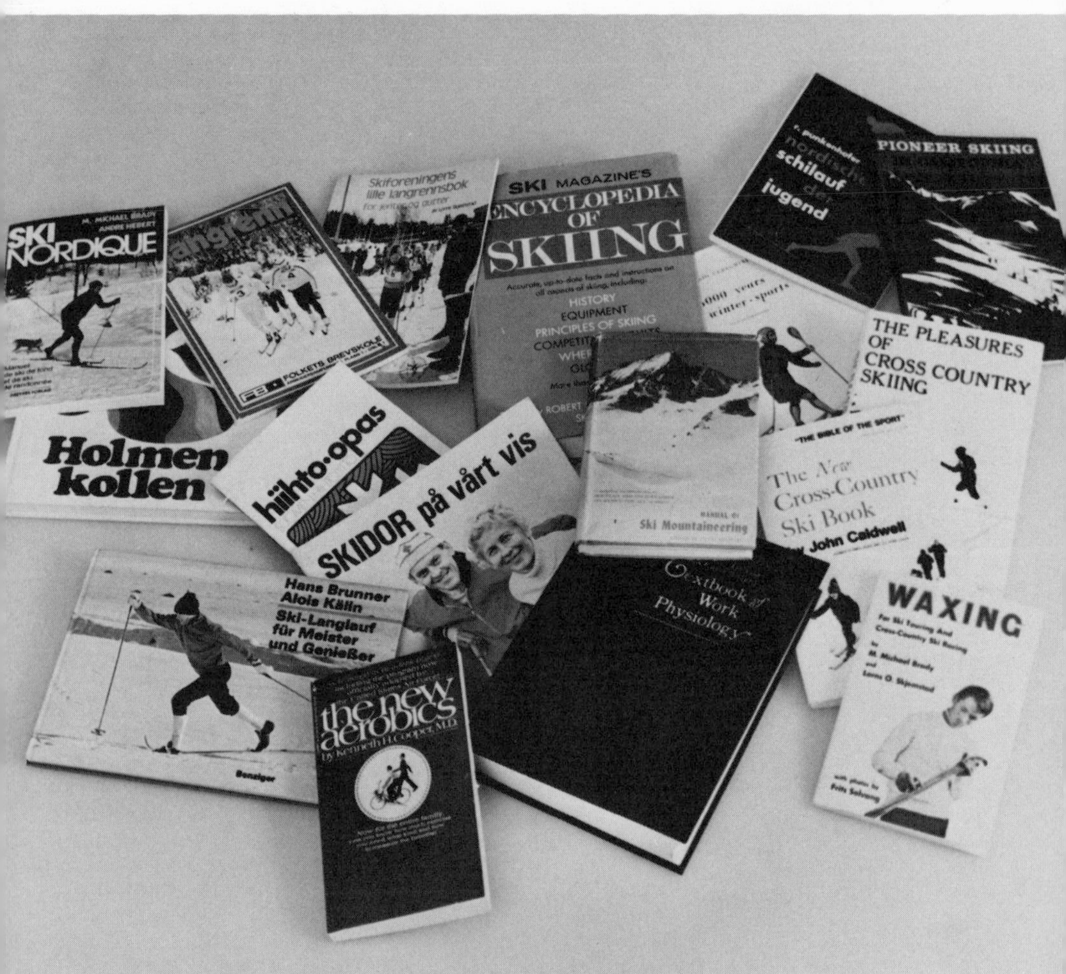
SKI NORDIQUE
M. MICHAEL BRADY
ANDRE HEBERT
langrenn
FOLKETS BREVSKOLE
Skiforeningens lille langrennsbok
SKI MAGAZINE'S
ENCYCLOPEDIA OF SKIING
HISTORY
EQUIPMENT
PRINCIPLES OF SKIING
schilauf
jugend
PIONEER SKIING
winter-sports
THE PLEASURES OF CROSS COUNTRY SKIING
Holmen kollen
hiihto-opas
SKIDOR på vårt vis
Ski Mountaineering
"THE BIBLE OF THE SPORT"
The New Cross-Country Ski Book
John Caldwell
Hans Brunner
Alois Kälin
Ski-Langlauf für Meister und Genießer
Benziger
Work Physiology
the new aerobics
WAXING
For Ski Touring And Cross-Country Ski Racing

Selected Literature

The literature of ski touring and cross-country ski racing is not immense, but sections of some libraries are devoted to the subject. No attempt is made to list all available works here, but rather only those in book or booklet form that the authors have found useful in their studies of the subject and in writing this book. For fields of subsidiary interest for most readers, such as training and physiology, only publications generally available in the United States and Canada are listed. However, major works on cross-country and ski history in other languages are listed for those who wish to delve into the subject.

Athletic Psychology

Cratty, Bryant J. *Psychology and Physical Activity.* Englewood Cliffs, N.J.: Prentice-Hall, 1968. 214 pages.

Singer, Robert N. *Motor Learning and Human Performance.* New York: Macmillan, 1968. 354 pages.

Physiology

Åstrand, Per-Olof. *Ergometry.* Varberg, Sweden: Monark-Crescent cycle manufacturers, 1965. 33 pages.

Åstrand, Per-Olof, and Rodal, Kaare. *Textbook of Work Physiology.* New York: McGraw-Hill, 1970. 669 pages.

Ricci, Benjamin. *Physiological Basis of Human Performance.* Philadelphia: Lea and Febiger, 1970. 299 pages.

Training and Fitness

Bowerman, William J., and Harris, W. E. *Jogging.* New York: Grosset & Dunlap, 1967. 127 pages.

Cooper, Kenneth H. *Aerobics.* New York: Bantam Books, 1968. 173 pages.

Cooper, Kenneth H. *The New Aerobics.* New York: Bantam Books, 1970. 191 pages.

Cerutty, Percy Wells. *Athletics, How to Become a Champion.* London: Stanley Paul, 1960. 190 pages.

Ski Touring and Cross-Country Ski Racing

English

Brady, M. Michael. *Nordic Touring and Cross-Country Skiing.* 3rd rev. ed. Oslo: Dreyers Forlag, 1971. 88 pages.

Caldwell, John. *The New Cross-Country Ski Book.* Brattleboro, Vt.: Stephen Greene Press, 1971. 128 pages.

Lund, Morten. *The Pleasures of Cross Country Skiing.* New York: Outerbridge & Lazard, 1972. 195 pages.

German

Amman, Hans. *Das Training des Ski-Langlaufers.* Bern: Schweizer Skiverband, 1965. 12 pages.

Baumann, Ernst. *Langlauf für alle, ein Büchlein über das Skilaufen.* Zürich: Füssli, 1967. 79 pages.

Brunner, Hans, and Kälin, Alois. *Ski-Langlauf für Meister und Geniesser.* Bern: Benzinger, 1969. 80 pages.

Drescher, Helmut. *Skiwandern.* Munich: BLV, 1970. 143 pages.

Punkenhofer, Robert. *Nordischer Skilauf der Jugend.* Vienna: Österreichischer Bundesverlag, 1969. 87 pages.

Reichert, Fritz, and Lorenz, Siegfried. *Skilanglauf Anleitung.* Berlin: Berlin Sportverlag, 1967. 105 pages.

Wöllzenmüller, Franz, and Pause, Walter. *Skilanglauf-Skiwandern.* Munich: BLV, 1970. 144 pages.

French

Brady, M. Michael. *Ski Nordique.* Montréal: Messageries du Jour, 1972. 100 pages.

FFS. *Mémento du Ski de Fond.* Paris: Fédération Française de Ski, 1962. 108 pages.

Robert, André, ed. *Enseignement Ski de Fond Discipline Nordique.* Montréal: Quebec Division Canadian Ski Association, 1971. Series of 13 ring-bound stenciled chapters.

Italian

Nilsson, Bengt Hermann. *Sciare Come Al Nord.* Milan: Sperling & Kupfer, 1967. 108 pages.

Finnish

Koskivuori, Hannu, et al. *Hiihto Opas.* Helsinki: Finnish Ski Association, 1970. 34 pages.

Norwegian

Höidal, Roar, et al. *B-kurs Langrenn.* Oslo: Folkets Brevskole, 1972. 113 pages.

Kvello, Kristen, et al. *Treningsprogram langrenn.* 2 vols. Oslo: Norwegian Ski Federation, 1972. 90 pages.

Skjemstad, Lorns O. *Skiforeningens lille langrennsbok for jenter og gutter.* Oslo: Gröndahl & Söns, 1972. 48 pages.

Swedish

Larsson, Lennart, et al. *Träningsråd i Länglöping.* Stockholm: Swedish Ski Association, 1967. 38 pages.

Matsbo, Martin; Wehlin, Sunne; and Öster, Lars. *Åk Skidor.* Stockholm: Bokförlaget Robert Larsson, 1970. 109 pages.

Rönnlund, Toini and Assar. *Skidor På Vårt Vis.* Bjästa, Sweden: CEWE Förlaget, 1971. 26 pages.

Ski Mountaineering

Tejada-Flores, Lito, and Steck, Allen. *Wilderness Skiing.* San Francisco and New York: Sierra Club Totebook, 1972. 310 pages.

Frohm, Gösta, and Rosén, Bo, eds. *Vita Friluftsboken.* Stockholm: Rabén & Sjögren, 1966. 288 pages (in Swedish).

Röed, Öistein. *Respekt for Fjellet.* Oslo: Aschehoug, 1956. 202 pages (in Norwegian).

Biathlon

Biathlon Committee, Norwegian Rifle Association. *Veiledning i Ski- og Skifelt-skyting.* Oslo: Det Frivillige Skyttervesen Utvalget for Skiskyting, 1966, with amendments of 1969. 55 pages (in Norwegian).

U.S. Army, *Handbook of Biathlon Training.* United States Modern Winter Biathlon Training Center, U.S. Army, Alaska, 1967. 47 pages.

Nordic Combined

Technical Committee for Nordic Combined of the Norwegian Ski Federation. *Treningsprogram for Kombinerte Löpere.* Oslo: Norwegian Ski Federation, 1971. 42 pages (in Norwegian).

Snow and Waxing

Bentley, W. A., and Humphreys, W. J. *Snow Crystals.* New York: McGraw-Hill, 1931, and Dover, 1962. 227 pages.

Brady, M. Michael, and Skjemstad, Lorns O. *Waxing for Ski Touring and Cross-Country Ski Racing.* San Fernando, Calif.: Eiger, 1971. 35 pages.

Shimbo, Masaki. "Friction on Snow of Ski Soles, Unwaxed and Waxed." Kinosita, Koreo. "The Physics of Skiing—Preliminary and General Survey." Two chapters in *Scientific Study of Skiing in Japan.* Tokyo: Hitachi, 1972. 141 pages.

Regulations

FIS. *The International Ski Competition Rules, Book II, Cross-Country and Nordic Combined Events.* Bern: FIS, 1971. 24 pages.

United States Eastern Amateur Ski Association. *Cross Country Rules.* Hanover, N.H.: USEASA, 1961. 14 pages.

Ski Encyclopedias

Lang, Serge. *Le Ski et Autres Sports d'Hiver.* Paris: Larousse, 1967. 416 pages (in French).

Scharff, Robert, and Editors of *Ski* Magazine. *Encyclopedia of Skiing.* New York: Harper & Row, 1970. 427 pages.

Ski History

Bö, Olav. *Skiing Traditions in Norway.* Oslo: Det Norske Samlaget, 1968. 126 pages.

Cereghini, Mario. *5000 Years of Winter Sports.* Milan: Edizioni Del Milione, 1955. 144 pages.

Lid, Nils. *On the History of Norwegian Skis.* Oslo: Gröndahl & Söns, 1937. 23 pages.

Power, Robert H. *Pioneer Skiing in California.* Vacaville, Calif.: Nut Tree, 1960. 26 pages.

Vaage, Jakob. *Holmenkollen.* Oslo: Norske Bokklubben, 1971. 255 pages (in Norwegian).

Vaage, Jakob. *Norske Ski Erobrer Verden.* Oslo: Gyldendal, 1952. 232 pages (in Norwegian).

Glossary of Terms Used in Ski Touring and Cross-Country Racing

Aerobic Literally "with air," term used to describe physiological processes requiring oxygen supply.

Aerobic capacity A measure of the ability to perform aerobic work over longer periods of time. Often expressed as maximum oxygen uptake.

Agility In touring skiing, the ability to use body flexibility in the most efficient manner.

Alpine skiing Recreational downhill skiing, and slalom, giant slalom, and downhill racing, originally developed in the Alps of Europe.

Anaerobic Literally "without air," term used to describe physiological processes capable of functioning without an oxygen supply.

Anaerobic capacity A measure of the body's capability to perform muscular work over and above the limit set by maximum oxygen uptake.

Anorak Lightweight shell parka, usually with a hood.

Arm trainers Various mechanisms designed to load arm muscles in training in the diagonal stride or double-pole rhythms.

Backslip Skis do not grip but slide backward, caused by improper wax or incorrect technique.

Backstrap binding Ski bindings consisting of a toepiece and a strap around the boot heel to hold the toe in the binding.

Bail Clamp-down piece on toe binding to hold boot sole against binding pegs.

Base preparation Compounds applies to wood ski bases for waterproofing and wax holding.

Base wax Waxes used "under" final waxes to increase durability.

Basket Round ring attached near bottom of ski pole, 3 to 5 inches in diameter, to prevent its sinking into the snow.

Biathlon A competitive Nordic skiing event combining cross-country skiing and rifle shooting.

Camber The arching of the middle of a ski up above its tip and tail, which distributes the skier's weight evenly over the ski.

Christiania Name of Oslo, Norway, until 1924. In skiing, the side-slipping phase of some downhill turns.

CISM Conseil International Militaire du Sport—the International Military Sports Council—organizers of military skiing competition.

Combined In Nordic competitive skiing, an event combining 15-km cross-country ski racing and ski jumping on a hill having a norm point of 60 to 70 meters.

Corn Large-grained snow, produced by settling, freezing, and thawing subsequent to falling.

Course The route followed by a cross-country ski race.

Cross-country The competitive form of ski touring. In common U.S. usage, the entirety of touring and cross-country skiing.

Crouch High-speed downhill position allowing the body to rest naturally in a position of readiness.

CSA The Canadian Ski Association. Headquarters: Room C–15, 306 Place d'Youville, Montreal 125, Quebec.

Diagonal stride Ski-touring stride in which opposite arm and leg move together, as in normal walking on foot.

Distance training Endurance training aimed at building up aerobic capacity.

Double poling Both arms and both poles move in unison.

Edge In skiing, refers to the edge of the ski bottom, or the use of these edges to gain control of skis.

Egg Compact high-speed downhill position having the least wind resistance.

Endurance The ability to perform prolonged work, such as cross-country racing, without fatigue.

Ergometer cycle A stationary cycle on which a subject pedals at a fixed speed against a fixed resistance. Used in measuring aerobic endurance.

Fall line The shortest line directly down a hill.

Fartslek From the Swedish; literally "speed game." A game form of interval and tempo training.

FIS Fédération Internationale de Ski—The International Ski Federation. Headquarters: Elfenstrasse 19, Bern 16, Switzerland.

Flexibility A measure of maximum physical movement such as how far in one direction you can bend.

Forward spring The characteristic of a touring ski to spring upward and forward when unweighted.

Glide The part of a ski touring stride when one or both skis are gliding, partially or fully weighted.

Grip (1) Skis "bite" into the snow giving foundation for the kick, (2) the handle of a ski pole.

Groove In a ski, a *tracking* groove in the ski bottom to make it run straight. In a boot, a *cable* groove in the boot heel to hold cable or strap of general touring bindings.

Grundvalla Swedish for "base wax." Poorly defined. May mean base preparation or base wax, depending on the manufacturer.

Hard wax Ski-touring wax for cold and dry to slightly wet snow. Comes in round foil cans holding 1½ to 2 ounces of wax.

Heel plates Plates mounted under the heel on the ski to dig into a weighted boot heel to keep it from slipping sideways off the ski.

Herringbone An uphill stride with ski tips spread to form a V, named for pattern skis make in snow.

Imitation training Movements performed on foot to imitate and thus teach skiing movements.

Impregnating Waterproofing process for wooden ski soles.

Interval training A series of intense but relatively short exercise periods separated from one another by rest intervals.

IOC The International Olympic Committee.

Kick As in walking, a backward thrusting toe push-off and leg extension that propels the skier forward in the touring strides.

Kick turn A stationary 180-degree turn performed by lifting and reversing direction of one ski, followed by the other ski.

Klister Tacky, fluid ski touring waxes for wet and/or settled snow. Wax comes in 2- to 4-ounce tubes.

Klister-wax Ski-touring wax for conditions near freezing. Comes in round foil cans holding 1½ to 2 ounces of wax.

Langlauf German for cross-country ski racing.

Light touring Ski-touring equipment closely resembling cross-country racing equipment, but stronger and slightly heavier.

Light track Touring trail or cross-country course illuminated for nighttime skiing.

Lignostone (from the Latin *lignum,* meaning wood) Beech wood compressed to half its original volume, used for ski edges.

Mountain Heaviest type of general-touring skis, intended for extensive mountain touring or polar exploration.

Muscular fitness The ability of the skeletal muscles to perform movements.

NAHSTA National Hiking and Ski Touring Association. Headquarters: Box 7421, Colorado Springs, Colorado 80918.

Natural stance Natural erect body position. In downhill skiing, the easiest and most erect position to assume.

Neswood Trade name for a plastic-impregnated hard wood used for touring ski bases. Needs no base preparation.

Nordic Geographically defines Norway, Sweden, and Finland. In skiing, defines recreational ski touring, competitive cross-country ski racing, ski jumping, Nordic combined, and Biathlon events.

Nordic Norm Standard stipulating boot and toe binding widths and sole side angles, and ski midpoint widths.

Orienteering A competitive event combining running on foot or cross-country ski racing with map reading.

Parallel turn Downhill turn made with skis parallel throughout the turn.

Passgang Obsolete touring stride in which arm and leg on one side move in unison.

Peg binding Ski-touring toe binding comprising aluminum

toepiece and a bail to press the boot toe down against two or three pegs extending upward from the toe plate.

Permagli Trade name for an impregnated laminated hard wood used for touring ski bases. Needs no base preparation.

Pole set The act of planting a pole in the snow.

Poling Arm movements with poles that supply forward power.

Pulk Small toboggan drawn by poles fixed to belt around waist of touring skier. Used for transporting provisions on extended tours and for children.

Pullover socks Rubber, rubberized nylon, or nylon-terrycloth socks pulled over cross-country or light-touring boots for additional waterproofing and warmth.

Relay A cross-country ski-racing team event: a four-man event covering 40 kilometers or a four-woman event covering 20 kilometers.

Resilience A component of muscular fitness. In ski touring, the ability to kick rapidly, to ascend hills rapidly, etc.

Roller skis Wheeled platforms attached to the foot with standard cross-country bindings and boots. Used in imitation training.

Rucksack Knapsack with a frame, especially suitable for ski touring.

Shovel Upturn part of the ski tip.

Side camber The concave curve on the side of a ski which makes the middle narrower than the tip or tail. Side camber aids ski tracking and turning.

Sideslip Skis gliding controlled sideways.

Skare General term for hard and/or icy crust on snow.

Skating turn A flat terrain or downhill turn executed by one or more skating steps in the new direction.

Ski striding A variation of walking or running done uphill on foot to imitate skiing movements.

Ski touring Recreational form of Nordic skiing.

Snowplow Downhill position for slowing down, stopping, and turning. Ski tips together, tails apart.

Snowplow turn Downhill turn executed in the snowplow position.

Sole Ski bottom.

Speed training Training aimed at attaining high speed.

STA Ski Touring Association. Headquarters: Box 9, West Simsbury, Connecticut 06092.

Stem Christiania Downhill turn initiated with a stem and finished with ski parallel and sideslipping through the fall line.

Stem turn Downhill turn in which one ski is stemmed, or angled out pointing in the direction of turn, and weighted to perform the turn.

Step test A test in which the subject steps up and down from a platform for a period of about 5 minutes, with pulse measured thereafter. Provides an indication of aerobic capacity.

Step turn A stationary or moving turn performed by stepping skis progressively around to the new direction.

Strength A component of muscular fitness. The ability to lift, push, or pull against a resistance.

Stride In skiing, the walklike leg and arm movements that propel the skier forward.

Tacking turn Uphill turn connecting two traverses, done in diagonal-stride rhythm.

Tail The back end of a ski.

Tar General term for tarlike base-preparation compounds. Tars are available in air-dry and warm-in compounds.

Telemark Region in South-central Norway. In skiing, a position with both knees bent, one leg trailing the other.

Telemark turn An older steered ski turn common when skis were heavier and bindings looser. Used infrequently in modern ski touring in deep snow; never used in cross-country ski racing.

Tempo training Running or skiing at racing speed for periods equalling 10 to 20 percent of a race's duration.

Tip The front end of a ski, or the bottom end of a ski pole.

Toe binding Ski bindings that attach the boot to the ski by clamping the front part of the boot welt to the binding.

Tonkin Treated bamboo, used for ski poles.

Torch Usually a butane- or propane-fueled blowtorch equipped with a flame spreader and a waxing iron attachment. Intended for assisting base preparation, application and removal of waxes.

Touring Ski touring. In equipment, the most common category of ski touring equipment.

Track In touring, the depressions left by skis in snow. In cross-country racing, the prepared tracks for a race.

Training Any physical activity that maintains or improves physical ability.

Traversing Skiing up or down a hill on a traverse at an angle to the fall line.

UIPM Union Internationale de Pentathlon Moderne. Name of UIPMB prior to 1968.

UIPMB Union Internationale de Pentathlon Moderne et Biathlon, the International Modern Pentathlon and Biathlon Association. Organizers of biathlon skiing competition.

USSA The United States Ski Association. Headquarters: 1726 Champa Street, Suite 300, Denver, Colorado 80202.

Waxing iron A metal block on a handle, to be heated for warming and smoothing out waxes.

Weight transfer Transfer of weight from one ski to the other. In motion, as in skiing, weight transfer also involves dynamic (due to motion) forces in addition to body weight.

Wide-track A stance in downhill skiing, skis parallel and 4 to 15 inches apart.

Index